[C H R I S T I A N   H O P E]

Christian Hope

BY BERNARD OLIVIER, O.P.

Translated by Paul Barrett, O.F.M.CAP.

THE NEWMAN PRESS
Westminster · Maryland
1963

Originally published by
La Pensée Catholique, Brussels, as
L'espérance Chrétienne.

Imprimi potest
FR. JACOBUS A MITCHELSTOWN, O.F.M.CAP.
Min. Prov. Hib.
September 4, 1961

Nihil obstat
JOHN F. DEDE, S.S., J.C.D.
Censor Deputatus

Imprimatur
LAWRENCE J. SHEHAN, D.D.
Archbishop of Baltimore
December 19, 1962

All rights reserved.
Library of Congress Catalog Card Number: 63-12233
Copyright © 1963 by THE NEWMAN PRESS
Printed in the United States of America
by H. Wolff, New York

Designed by Leda Arensberg

Preface

✠

"Hope, little hope, moves forward between her two big sisters and no one even notices her."

CHARLES PEGUY

Hope, that little damsel so dear to Péguy, has fallen ill in our world: she is pining away and may be dying. Or perhaps it would be more accurate to say that it is our world that is pining away because it has paid no attention to hope. Literature has become dismal, and Péguy seems to be raving about impossible dreams. Even Catholics sometimes cultivate a dark pessimism because it is fashionable to be pessimistic now, just as pining away for love used to be the thing to do in the romantic era. Yet it is true that the world of today scarcely inspires joy, and even the best of men may be tempted to wonder where it will all end.

Still, as the embers of a fire may remain hidden for a long time beneath the ashes only to burst once more into bright flame, so, too, is true hope always present, ready to shine out to light the path, and nothing will quench it because it comes from God and returns to Him. Hope is a divine force which no human misery can hold in check and which begets joy even in suffering, persecution, injustice, and failure. It changes night into day and tears into laughter, not by any kind of magic spell, but simply because it is a divine, living, and irresistible reality. It must be restored to the world, for it is what the world lacks most.

These pages have no other aim than to help Catholics understand better the real meaning of Christian hope and perhaps to introduce into their everyday lives and into the world at large this great liberating force.

We dedicate this book especially to those who have lost courage because they have forgotten that God loves them, and also to those who confuse mere gloominess with great tragedy.

Contents

✠

[C H R I S T I A N   H O P E]

··❧[1]❧··

The Nature of Hope

✠

As every Catholic knows, hope is one of the three theological virtues. Created by God in our souls at the same
time as grace and all the gifts that accompany it, hope enables us to do certain definite interior acts which are of
vital importance to us as Christians and which reach out
directly to God as their object. Revelation teaches us about
the reality and exact scope of this virtue, and hence, if we
wish to understand it, we must seek the answers especially
in Scripture.

However, when God speaks to men and reveals to them
some mystery, He does so in terms that they can grasp and
He uses ideas that they can understand. Thus when He
wished to teach us about charity, He had recourse to the
idea of love, with which all of us are familiar. In like man-

ner, since He wishes to tell us about the virtue of hope, we know that it has something in common with those feelings of hope which we experience in our daily lives. Accordingly, if we wish to grasp fully the nature of revealed hope, we must begin with the concept of merely human hope.[1]

MAN LIVES BY HOPE

If we examine the texture of our lives, we shall be surprised to find how necessary hope is to us. We just cannot live without it; and every day we are sustained by hopes of all kinds. We are always hoping—that the next day will be fine, that a friend will be home when we call, that there will be no war. Hope enables the sick man to bear his pains and gives him the strength to fight; it gives us patience under trial and helps us to persevere in our endeavors. If it weren't for our daily hopes, would we have the strength to keep on living? There is certainly much wisdom in the old saying, "While there's life, there's hope."

More fundamentally still, we need hope to be able to look calmly and with assurance at life itself. In this world we are buffeted unceasingly and tossed about by the tides of fortune; we advance and retreat; we are torn and divided. Hence if we are to bear all this with courage, we must have the firm hope that it serves some purpose, that it leads somewhere. And if we are not to lose heart when we see the immense burden of suffering that presses down upon humanity and the discouraging success of evil in the

[1] There is a very complete, and very personal, phenomenological study of hope in G. Marcel's *Homo Viator*.

world, we need the assured hope that man has a destiny, a final end, which, when it is attained, will justify in some mysterious way the incomprehensible realities of life. An absurd world in which nothing makes sense, in which nothing is certain, can beget only despair, that dreary resignation to an inability to solve the essential problem of man's destiny.

Thus in our lives hope is a sign of our weakness and, at the same time, a driving force. It reveals our weakness because it shows that the realization of our prospects and desires does not depend wholly upon ourselves, that we lack something without which we cannot succeed and for which, consequently, we are compelled to hope. But hope is also a great force in our lives. The more firmly founded it is and the more we can support ourselves upon it, the more it becomes a prop for our weakness and a help to our feeble strength. It provides us with the assurance which we cannot find within ourselves.

Just as hope plays such an indispensable role in merely human affairs, so, too, is it needed in the Christian life. As the natural man lives by natural hope, so does the Christian live by Christian hope and cannot survive without it. The psychological characteristics of the man who is sustained by merely human hope are found also, but on a more essential level, in him who is sustained by Christian hope.

THE ROLE OF HOPE IN MAN'S EMOTIONAL LIFE

Like all other "passions," hope originates in the affective part of our nature. It is one of the movements of our appe-

titive faculty when that faculty is confronted with some
good. When some good, some desirable object (desirable
in the literal sense) is presented to us, it instinctively arouses
in us a movement of *love*. This movement is the first and
immediate reaction of our "appetite" in the presence of
anything desirable. But love is the germ of all "passion," for
scarcely is love born, when it wants to conquer, and it fulfills itself only when it possesses the thing that is loved. Thus
the whole of man's affective life lies between love, which is
its beginning, and the pleasure of enjoyment, which is its
culminating point.

But it is not always possible to pass directly from love to
enjoyment, for the thing that we love may not belong to
us, at least not yet. In that case, *desire* intervenes between
love and the perfect joy of possession; with all our hearts
we reach out to the object we love and we long to possess
it. However, desiring is one thing while possessing is quite
another, and there are usually many obstacles between the
one and the other. Our fairy tales abound in dragons and
giants whom the knight must vanquish before he can
marry the princess of his dreams. So, too, the presence of
obstacles in our path injects an element of uncertainty into
our desire, and we wonder if we shall be able to surmount
the barriers that confront us. At this point, under the pres-
sure of a desire that must be satisfied despite everything,
we experience the stirring of the fighting spirit, of that
"drawing-up of the soul," of which St. Bonaventure speaks.
There is a battle to be fought, a citadel to be stormed, and
our success depends on the means at our disposal. It is here
that *hope* arises or despair is born.

If, despite the powerful impetus that is carrying us toward our desired object, we feel that we cannot reach our goal because we lack the means required, then we experience despair, that fearful lack of inner strength which is all the worse the stronger and more clearly defined has been our desire. With all our heart we have longed to possess the thing we love and then suddenly we are forced to admit that we shall never reach it. But if, on the contrary, despite all difficulties, despite the uncertainty that persists until we attain our object, we are convinced that we shall succeed because we are assured of adequate support, then hope springs up in our hearts, it carries us over all obstacles and begets in us a deep, patient and unshakable confidence. Hence the decisive element in hope, that which makes hope possible, is the efficacy of the means to the end, the value of the support upon which it is founded.

PORTRAIT OF THE HOPEFUL MAN

Therefore we can describe the hopeful man as follows:

1) He is one who is in love, who has not yet attained the object of his love and who is still reaching out to it in desire. This desire entails and is fed by a real feeling of deprivation and want. The satisfied man, or he who regards himself as such, no longer desires anything, for he is content with what he has, and, in his own mind at least, he is rich. Hence he is at the opposite pole from the hopeful man because he who desires nothing can hope for nothing. On the contrary, however, he who has sounded the void within

him, who feels the emptiness of a love still unfulfilled, is keenly conscious of his need and is ripe for hope.[2]

2) The hopeful man is completely turned toward the future. His perfect joy is neither in the past nor the present but is still to come and consists only in the possession of the good he covets. All his desires are centered on the object he loves, and for which he is waiting expectantly and fervently. Unlike the satisfied man, he does not sit back contentedly, placidly savoring his happiness, for he knows that he has still to bring out the best in him. He lives for the future, not the present, and this, perhaps, is the true mark of those who are young in heart.

3) The hopeful man is a *fighting man*. Hitherto we have identified the hopeful man as a man of desires. But there is a difference between merely desiring and actively fighting to get what one desires, and it is the obstacle or obstacles separating desire from possession that make the difference. Hope presupposes an urge to overcome such obstacles. The hopeful man is not content merely to gaze from afar on his goal, but instead he faces up to any barrier that may lie between him and it. He is in a state of permanent struggle. Yet, despite the element of uncertainty caused by the presence of an obstacle, he is sure that he will win, and his assuredness is based on the efficacy of the means he has at his disposal, which can come to him from outside himself. That is the true and somewhat paradoxical nature of hope, a firm, basic core of confidence surrounded by uncertainty, for without the continued danger of defeat there would be no real hope but only a serene interval of confident wait-

[2] From this we can see why the kingdom of heaven, which is the object of Christian hope, belongs to the poor in spirit.

ing, a simple acceptance of an unavoidable delay. There-fore, the whole strength of hope, its whole potential of confidence, is linked to the means of overcoming obstacles, and it is the nature of this means that regulates the degree of confidence and the true quality of hope.

FROM HUMAN HOPE TO CHRISTIAN HOPE

All of the above psychological characteristics of human hope are to be found in Christian hope. The fact that hope is a theological virtue should not make us forget that, in a real sense, God's gifts become incarnate, that they are received by the whole man. Although man's theological life is supernatural, it is still not a life apart from his natural life, for as the classical adage says, grace does not destroy nature but heals, raises, and perfects it. Thus, although its object is essentially supernatural and not merely material, Christian hope is not for that reason to be reduced to the category of passionless or theoretical wishes. Rather it turns all man's strength, passions, and energy toward its supernatural object. The sad thing, however, is that, as St. Paul would say, we are often much less impassioned for the things that are above than we are for the things that are below, for invisible things than for those that are visible.

On the other hand, however, the transition from human to supernatural hope is not made simply by raising man's instinctive aspirations to a higher degree. Christian hope is not a sublimation of man's lower desires, but is a completely new reality pertaining to the world of grace, that is, to the free, supernatural gifts of God, wherein God alone can take the initiative. Only He can give us hope; only He can give us the object of Christian hope and start the inner movement of our whole being toward that object. Just as no human argument can beget that true faith which is the free gift of God, and just as no purely human affection can become true charity without His grace, so, too, Christian hope is not possible without His gift. That is why, if we want to understand the nature of hope, we must search for it in God's revelation.

2

The Old Testament

✠

God's redemption of the world has a history since it took place in time and followed a certain sequence. Like everything else that concerns men on this earth, redemption had a beginning, it progressed, and it reached its culminating point. It is the realization, in human history, of the eternal plan, of that mystery hidden in God since before the beginning of time.

Hope, like faith, has its history, too. God did not reveal Himself all at once; He did not decree that men should have a finished faith from the very first day of his existence, but instead He followed a plan of slow and progressively expanding enlightenment. For instance, even such a basic doctrine as the Blessed Trinity was unknown in the Old Testament and was revealed clearly only in Christ.

So it was also with hope. God did not reveal it fully from the beginning, but accommodated Himself to man's condition, which required a gradual unfolding of the doctrine of hope over the years. He gave the first impetus to the great hope that was to travel down through the ages until the end of the world, but He revealed that hope only little by little as He led men along step by step until they were able to understand it and participate in it. He knew where He was leading men but He made their destination known to them only by degrees. The whole history of the Chosen Race is the primitive history of hope; it is the history of a people that was marching toward the realization of a real hope—the Messianic Kingdom of God.

THE JOURNEY TOWARD THE PROMISE

Hope is the underlying and supporting theme of the whole of the Old Testament, and the history of Israel is like a veritable incarnation of hope.

Israel was born of a summons, a vocation, and even before it was made a separate nation, it was assigned a goal. Unlike other nations, it had no past, no tradition to justify its existence as a distinct entity, but was a nation, perhaps the only nation in history, whose whole reason for existence lay in its future. The history of Israel began with a divine call, for God had a plan which He wished to fulfil in and by the Israelites after a long period of development. That is why from the start He put the seal of vocation upon the first small clan and upon the budding race and guided them toward a goal which He alone knew fully. He revealed this goal gradually, and all the long patience of a divine teacher was needed to show Israel the real meaning of its destiny. It is true that everything was contained in germ in the original promise which God made to Abraham, but the whole of the divine plan was not to be unfolded until the appointed time. Israel was to grope blindly toward a goal which it did not even dream existed, or rather, the Chosen Race was like an impatient shortsighted traveller who was unable and unwilling to look beyond the next stage of his journey. God took the Israelites as they were and did not hold out to them all at once the complete and essential hope He had in store for them. Instead, He offered it to them piece by piece, leading them on from one desire to another, from one hope to another, toward the object of true hope. All of the Old Testament is the history of the advance of a race who knew they were called, guided, and sustained by God. It is the story of an immense aspiration which, though often temporarily satisfied, still went surging on to new goals, beyond which the definitive object of all the Jews' hopes, the kingdom of God in the Messianic era, was to appear in its own time.

This characteristic climate of hope was apparent from the time of the basic event in the life of Israel, namely, the calling of Abraham. God, as it were, broke in upon Abraham's life, drew him away from his familiar surroundings to act as an instrument in the divine plan, and made him a binding promise: "I will make a great nation of you. I will bless you, and make your name great" (Gen. 12:2). Later God renewed this promise even more solemnly still when He said to Abraham: "Look at the heavens and, if you can, count the stars. . . . So shall your posterity be" (Gen.

15:5). Abraham took God at His word, believed with that faith which made him a just man, and, at the same time, entered the stream of hope.

God's intervention made Abraham a different man. Separated from his tribe and in exile from his homeland, the patriarch had his eyes fixed only on the future. He had become the man of the Covenant, the man of the Promise. The word of Yahweh had set before him a goal which exerted a powerful attraction on him, for we must remember how precious to ancient peoples was the promise of a numerous posterity. Abraham was not yet able even to suspect all that lay behind the immediate promise, but the promise itself was enough to engender that confident expectation that today still lives in the heart of the Christian.

At the time the promise was made to him, Abraham had, in the course of nature, little prospect of ever reaching the object of his desire because his wife, Sara, was barren. Thus human circumstances seemed to make his goal inaccessible. In other words, for Abraham, there was an obstacle between desire and possession, and therefore he had to rely solely on God's word. His willingness to wait for the fulfillment of the promise, even to reach out for it, was an act of total abandonment to God, who had made the promise. Hope is possible only when one trusts oneself unconditionally to Him who is faithful to His promises. Such is the living complex of elements that go to make up the simplest act of hope.

When God further tested Abraham by commanding him to sacrifice Isaac, He gave him, the father of believers, the chance to prove his unshakable faith and to show the strength of his hope in the face of the impossible, even the absurd. Hence, Abraham is rightly called the father of those who hope. In him the history of the Jewish people, the people of the promise, was already summed up.

THE STAGES OF HOPE

1. The Initial Promise

Although its precise object was *Abraham's posterity*, God's promise was made in terms that allowed of an extension far beyond the prophecy of a mere line of descendants such as an ordinary man could expect: "I will make a great nation of you. I will bless you, and make your name great, so that you shall be a blessing. I will bless them that bless you, and curse them that curse you. In you shall all the nations of the earth be blessed" (Gen. 12:2–3).

Thus, the object of the first promise contained in germ the whole development of the story of salvation. The first and most immediate fruits of the promise were soon granted, and in their turn, Isaac and Jacob were encouraged to hope as Abraham did. So, from the days of Jacob onward, the sacred author was able to enumerate an already numerous posterity, the roots from which the twelve tribes of Israel were to grow.

2. The Promised Land

A second special object, the Promised Land, was added to the first. These two words, "Promised Land," contain the great aspiration of the first Israelites; they described a tangible sign of the Covenant between God and His Chosen

People, of the solemn pact which Yahweh would never belie:

> The Lord appeared to Abraham and said: "To your descendants I will give this land. . . . This is my covenant with you: You shall be the father of a multitude of nations; you shall no longer be called Abram, but your name shall be Abraham; for I will make you the father of a multitude of nations. I will make you exceedingly fruitful; I will make nations of you, and kings shall descend from you. I will establish my covenant between you and me and your descendants after you throughout their generations, as a perpetual covenant, that I may be a God to you and to your descendants after you. I will give you and your descendants after you this land in which you are immigrants, all the land of Chanaan as a perpetual possession, and I will be their God" (Gen. 12:7, 17:4–8).

The most memorable events in the ancient history of Israel are but the great stages in the fulfilling of this promise —the exodus from Egypt, the passage through the Red Sea, the wanderings in the desert, the crossing of the Jordan, and finally the gradual conquest of the cities of Canaan.

Yahweh's faithful granting of all that He had promised strengthened the Israelites' confidence in His word. From the living memory of His promise, this mere handful of people drew the courage to stand up to superior armies and powerful nations in defense of their homeland. As they fought to preserve the land which had been promised to them and which they now possessed, the Israelites were always conscious of being protected by the Promise.

Nevertheless, once they had established themselves in their new country, the Israelites were in danger of becoming self-complacent, attributing all their success to their own efforts. They still expected the wonderful destiny that was announced to them, but meanwhile they forgot the humility and the sense of poverty and need that must characterize hope. They awaited the Day of the Lord, which they imagined would come as a ringing proclamation of God's special love for them and as an era wherein they would be greater than all other nations. But, one after the other, the prophets came to cast their reproaches and threats in the face of a guilty people, warning them that the Day of the Lord would be a fearsome one for Israel because they would be judged according to their sins. The climax of God's chastisement of His Chosen People finally came in the Babylonian exile.

3. The Return to Jerusalem

Then in the midst of the ruins, hope was reborn. All of this had been foretold. God was punishing them and, if they repented, He would listen to them. A new goal was proposed to them—deliverance, salvation and *return to their homeland*. The voices of the prophets were raised in encouragement:

And I will gather together the remnant of my flock, out of all the lands into which I have cast them out; and I will make them return to their own fields, and they shall increase and be multiplied. And I will set up pastors over them, and they shall feed them: they shall fear no more, and they shall not be dismayed, and none shall be wanting of their number, saith the Lord. Behold the days come, saith the Lord, and I will raise up to David a just branch; and a king shall reign, and shall be wise; and shall execute judgment and justice in

the earth. In those days Juda shall be saved, and Israel shall
dwell confidently. And this is the name that they shall call
him: The Lord Our Just One. Therefore behold the days
come, saith the Lord, and they shall say no more: The Lord
liveth, who brought up the children of Israel out of the land
of Egypt, but, The Lord liveth, who hath brought out, and
brought hither the seed of the house of Israel from the land
of the north, and out of all the lands, to which I had cast
them forth; and they shall dwell in their own land (Jer.
23:3–8).

Isaias and Ezechiel also loved to describe the return of
the Israelites to their own country, the restoration of divine
worship and the new city (Isa. 40, 41, 44, 45; Ez. 36, 40,
etc.).

4. The Messianic Era

Finally, the ultimate object for which Israel was to hope,
the Messianic era, began to appear with growing insistence.
It is not easy to trace exactly the development of the Messianic idea among the Hebrews for it is extremely complex.
Perhaps the best way to describe it would be to say that
it resembles a mosaic of images placed side by side.

The mysterious event had already been announced in
God's blessing of Abraham and also in Jacob's blessing of
his sons, in which Juda was marked off from his brothers.
Later the Messianic idea was made more precise in David,
but still it remained blurred, and only in the prophets did it
gradually begin to assume capital importance.

Before the Babylonian exile, Isaias, the prophet of the
Messias, was the principal herald of the wonderful era to
come, and his Messianic texts are among the best known,

for example, the virgin who would conceive, the "Emmanuel" prophecy, or the text used in the Christmas liturgy:

> The people that walked in darkness, have seen a great light. To them that dwelt in the region of the shadow of death, light is risen. . . . For a child is born to us, and a son is given to us, and the government is upon his shoulder: and his name shall be called, Wonderful, Counsellor, God the Mighty, the Father of the world to come, the Prince of Peace. His empire shall be multiplied, and there shall be no end of peace. He shall sit upon the throne of David, and upon his kingdom: to establish it and strengthen it with judgment and with justice, from henceforth and forever (Isa. 9:2, 6–7).

He describes the peace and prosperity of this blessed time with remarkable lyricism:

> The wolf shall dwell with the lamb, and the leopard shall lie down with the kid. The calf and the lion and the sheep shall abide together, and a little child shall lead them. The calf and the bear shall feed; their young ones shall rest together; and the lion shall eat straw like the ox. And the suckling child shall play on the hole of the asp; and the weaned child shall thrust his hand into the den of the basilisk (Isa. 11:6–8).

Often the announcement of the Messianic kingdom is mingled with that of the return from exile, and the events are presented in such a perspective that it is sometimes difficult to distinguish between them. In general, however, the return to Jerusalem was apparently to coincide with the establishment of the definitive rule of Yahweh (Jer. 30–31), but sometimes it was even equated with the coming of the eschatological kingdom, and was thus identified with the "end of time" (Ez. 38–39; Isa. 41ff.).

But even after the entry into Jerusalem, and despite the restoration and the rebuilding of the Temple, the promises had still to be fulfilled. That glorious kingdom marked by widespread peace, abundance and happiness, was still in the future. Once more the prophets raised their voices to proclaim that the kingdom of God was at hand, an announcement that was to echo through the last centuries of expectancy and with which John the Baptist would inaugurate the New Testament.

How did the Hebrews envision this Messianic era? It's hard for us to say, because they themselves had not a very clear idea of it. In general, though, we can distinguish three elements in it:

a) The prophets proclaimed the nearness of the *day of the Lord*, an event of the greatest importance but the exact nature of which remained quite vague. Most of the descriptions of this day surround it with a climate of terror—the day of the Lord was to be a fearful one, a day of mourning and not of joy. Nevertheless in the end it was to be beneficial to Israel, or at least to the small remnant of the nation that would be saved from destruction (cf. Aggeus, Zacharias, Abdias).[1]

b) The day of the Lord was to mark the establishment of the *Kingdom of God*. But the testimonies of the prophets were not in perfect agreement even on this point. Was the inauguration of this kingdom to be accomplished in an upheaval of the whole existing order, or was it to be, on the contrary, the final stage of a normal, peaceful evo-

[1] Apparently this Jewish conception of "the day of the Lord" can be compared to the Communists' idea of "*the* day" which so dominates their philosophy.

lution? In the opinion of M. J. Lagrange,[2] the majority of the texts tend to consider the inauguration as a passing from a state of law to a state of fact. By right God has always had dominion, not only over Israel, but also over all the nations of the earth, and His kingdom consists essentially in all mankind's acknowledgment of this divine right. This general recognition of God's rights would begin the new era of peace and happiness in which Israel would finally occupy among all nations the pre-eminence that was hers as a result of the divine predilection.

But when we consider the pertinent texts from apocalyptic literature, of which the Book of Daniel is an outstanding example among the canonical texts, the perspective changes.[3] Here the establishment of the kingdom appears as a sudden and clean break in the normal, foreseeable development of history, just as a general upheaval will mark the end of the world. In such an atmosphere, the kingdom of God takes on a clearly eschatological character: God will exercise His dominion especially over the elect in a new world.

c) Finally, the *Messias* is the one chosen by Yahweh as the divine instrument in establishing the kingdom. The Messias is generally depicted as a wise, powerful and glorious king. He is to come from the line of David and will therefore bestow on the ancient royal house an un-

---

[2] M. J. Lagrange, *Le Regne de Dieu dans l'Ancien Testament*, in *Revue Biblique*, 1908, pp. 36–61.

[3] The apocalyptic type of literature (which is one of the literary forms used in the Bible) is characterized particularly by a distinctly eschatological bent, for its purpose is to predict the events at the end of time. This literary form was developed principally in the apocryphal writings and it is frequently noteworthy for its esoteric atmosphere.

dying luster. The prophet Micheas even specified that he would be born in Bethlehem. Isaias alone foretold the sufferings and the supreme sacrifice of the "Servant" (Isa. 53), but this untraditional and disconcerting aspect of the personality of the Messias was left in the shadows, and the image that prevailed was the one that corresponded most with the aspirations of a people that was still very earthbound and materialistic, the image of a glorious king setting up a kingdom of abundance and prosperity.

The hopes of the whole people were fastened on this glorious era. They longed to see it appear, and each one hoped to be part of the generation chosen from all the rest to be alive at that moment. Happy would they be who would see those days with their own eyes! Hence there was a *common national hope* centered on a Messianic reign that was most often regarded as being historical and temporal. No doubt many generations would come and go before the kingdom began; yet, although they would not have the happiness of actually living in the Messianic era, it was nevertheless their duty to hope and wait because they, like all the other generations of Israel, belonged to the people of the Promise.

Hence, *purely individual hopes* for the coming of the Messias were put in second place [4] because it was to the

---

[4] Just as a sense of community exists only in the consciousness of the individual in the community, so, too, this "collective" hope really existed only in the hearts of individuals. Hence it can be called an *individual* hope. But the object of the Jews' hope had a clearly communal character because the thing they hoped for was not so much their own personal happiness as the realization of the destiny of their whole race which had been selected for the coming of the Messianic Kingdom of God.

Chosen Race as such, and to it alone, that the promise had been made.

Nevertheless, the problem of personal reward confronted the Jews, and they were far from solving it immediately. Most often, the just man looked forward to a completely material prosperity, to full granaries and an honorable old age, as the reward for his virtue. In fact, the average Jew was so convinced of this that he believed that anyone who had to undergo trials and tribulations was necessarily in a state of sin. (This line of argument runs through the Book of Job.) In the depths beyond the grave lay a vaguely defined place called *Sheol*, and the idea of happiness in a future life as a result of the resurrection of the body appeared very late. Isaias was the witness of this hope:

"Thy dead men shall live, my slain shall rise again. Awake, and give praise, ye that dwell in the dust. For thy dew is the dew of the light . . . , and the earth shall disclose her blood, and shall cover her slain no more" (Isa. 26:19–20).

It is especially in the Book of Machabees (second century B.C.) that we find vigorous expression of the hope for the resurrection of the body.[5] But in general we find no close connection between a future life, the reward for personal merit, and the Messianic era, the object of God's promise. In fact, the two ideas appear as completely separate from each other. Only in apocalyptic literature do we see the kingdom of God depicted as the exercise of divine

[5] See 2 Mach. 7, the account of the martyrdom of the seven brothers and their mother, each of whom in turn expressed faith in the resurrection; and 2 Mach. 12: 43–46, where Judas Machabeus, "thinking well and religiously concerning the resurrection," collects funds for an expiatory sacrifice on behalf of the dead soldiers.

dominion over a kingdom beyond the grave, a kingdom in which the just will share after the resurrection (see Daniel 12:1ff.). Belief in an immortality inaugurated by the resurrection was far from being as universal as belief in the coming of the Messias. The latter was imposed on everyone, although in different forms, even at the time of Christ, but the Sadducees, who drew their numbers mainly from the upper ranks of the priesthood, always denied the resurrection.

We can see from this how much the Jews had still to learn. The coming of Christ, fulfilling the words of the prophets and bringing the oracles to pass, was needed to release the real, spiritual meaning of the promise from the prosaic and very materialistic limits of Jewish traditions.

Such were, in broad outline, the successive stages through which Israel was led toward the great expectancy of the coming of the Messias. We can see now, in the light of Christ's revelation, that the objects proposed one after the other to the Jews were part of an over-all plan for carrying out God's designs. The Spirit of God worked tirelessly at His task, enticing Israel to progress step by step. He led these rough men along by holding out to them hopes that were suited to their capacity, guiding them toward that which was to be the supreme object of their desire. The immediate, material hopes which He held out to the Chosen Race kept them in a state of suspense and caused them to push on from one stage to another toward the real, supreme hope. Just as David and Cyrus can be considered as prophetic types and figures of the Messias, so the numberless posterity promised to Abraham, the Promised Land, and the return to Jerusalem, are like so many milestones marking the Jews' progress toward the essential object that lay beyond, namely, the expectation of the Messias.

THE FOUNDATION OF HOPE

Upon what foundation was hope built in the Old Testament? As we have seen, it was founded essentially on faith, which alone allows hope to be born. Yet there were other, more specific bases for hope.

God's numerous communications to man, especially the one given on Sinai, had struck deep into the hearts of the people because of the holy fear which His manifesting Himself always produced, and because of the Jews' consciousness of Yahweh's absolute transcendence and sovereign omnipotence. God alone was the Lord, the Holy One, the terrible, and no power could prevail against Him. "Whatsoever He willed, that He did." On the other hand, although His omnipotence set Him completely apart from all His creatures, He did not wish to remain withdrawn in His inaccessible majesty but rather willed to play a part in men's lives. Hence He chose Israel as His people, concluded an alliance with them and bound Himself to them with bonds of love. The God whom they feared and respected so much showed them that He was also a Father whose kindness was infinite and whose tenderness toward them was without parallel: "Can a woman forget her infant, so as not to have pity on the son of her womb? And if she should forget, yet I will not forget thee. Behold, I have graven thee in my hands . . ." (Isa. 49:15–16). These

were the deep roots of Israel's hope. The Jews, conscious
of their weakness and helplessness, knew that they had to
trust themselves completely to God's mercy. They relied
on His generosity for everything, for they knew that He
was omnipotent and that He had a special love for them.
This absolute confidence in God, based on His omnipotence and infinite kindness, inspired David to compose
many Psalms, among which are some of the most beautiful
songs ever written. All through the Book of Psalms, we
find this fundamental element of hope and unshakable confidence magnificently expressed:

> The Lord is my shepherd: I want for nothing; in green pas-
> tures he makes me lie down. He leads me to waters where I
> may rest; he gives refreshment to my soul (Ps. 23:1–2).
> The Lord is my light and my salvation; whom shall I fear?
> The Lord is the fortress of my life; of whom shall I be in
> dread . . . ?
> If a camp be pitched against me, my heart shall not fear;
> If a war should arise against me, I will be confident (Ps.
> 27:1, 3).

Yet the fact that God is omnipotent and kind is no absolute guarantee that He will fulfill a specific hope. Rather,
His power and goodness are but the foundations for a general indeterminate hope, and before we can confidently
await a definite object from God's hands, He must have
committed Himself to giving it, that is, He must have promised it to us. Hence, God's formal promise was the immediate motive for Israel's hope.

This is evident throughout the Old Testament. Yahweh
Himself invoked both His promise and His fidelity thereto: "I will fulfill the oath which I swore to your father

Abraham" (Gen. 23:3).[6] Moses, too, often recalled that the hopes of his "stiff-necked people" were based solely on God's promise and not on their own merits.[7] And when the prophets mingled a song of hope with their imprecations and threats, they were always referring to the divine promise and to God's fidelity to His word:

"For my name's sake I will remove my wrath far off; and for my praise I will bridle thee, lest thou shouldst perish" (Isa. 48:9). "Surely Ephraim is an honorable son to me, surely he is a tender child, for since I spoke of him, I will still remember him" (Jer. 31:20). Thus God's promise and His fidelity to it as proved by His numerous interventions on behalf of His Chosen Race, whom He saved with "His mighty extended arm," were the solid foundation of Israel's hope.

That, in broad outline, was the great movement which, supported by God alone, led the Jews from one stage to the other in the Old Testament. They were still groping along, seeking the real object of their hope, yet God guided them by the paths which He had marked out. Only in the revelation of Christ were they to find their goal, or as St. Paul says in his Epistle to the Hebrews (7:18–19): ". . . [the] bringing in of a better hope . . ."

[6] See also Gen. 17:1, 28:13–15, 48:3–4, etc.
[7] See Deut. 7:8, 8:1, 9:5, 9, 26–27, etc.

3

The New Testament

✠

THE SYNOPTIC GOSPELS

The word *elpis*, meaning "hope," is not found in the
Synoptic Gospels, a fact which at first sight may seem
strange. However, the omission is understandable when we
remember that with the word *pistis* ("faith"), the Synoptic
authors expressed both the idea of hope and the idea of
faith. In fact, in the Synoptic Gospels, faith is almost
always accompanied by that feeling of confidence in God
and absolute abandonment to His care which we associate
with the idea of hope. Indeed, faith, properly so-called, has
a very close connection with hope because belief in Christ
primarily means acknowledging Him as God's envoy, as the
Messias; and this is to acknowledge that He is the object

of the Jewish people's hope and that He personifies the great hope of the Old Testament. Hence, although the Synoptic authors do not use the actual word "hope," they certainly do express the reality.

1. The New Hope

When our Lord presented Himself as the Messias, He put an end to the Jews' age-long but mistaken expectations. Was there then nothing left to them to hope for? Indeed there was, because their hope, far from being destroyed, assumed its true form and became a "better hope," for Christ had come to inaugurate the kingdom of God which they were so eagerly awaiting. However, they did have a wrong idea about the nature of this kingdom, which is not surprising, for Christ Himself called the kingdom of God a "mystery" (Mark 4:11, Matt. 13:11, Luke 8:10). Hence He had to proceed patiently. Yet His efforts did not meet with easy success, for the idea of a temporal and material kingdom was deeply rooted in the minds of the Jews. Thus after the first multiplication of the loaves they wanted to carry Him off to make Him king. Still later, they regarded His triumphal entry into Jerusalem on Palm Sunday as somewhat of a march on the city. And even just before the Ascension, one of His disciples asked Him earnestly: "Lord, wilt thou at this time restore the kingdom of Israel?" (Acts 1:6).

Therefore, our Lord had to make first His disciples and then the people at large understand that He had indeed come to establish the kingdom of God, but that it was a *spiritual* kingdom. From the time of His Sermon on the Mount, the conditions which He laid down for entry into the kingdom placed heavy stress on this spiritual character. For example, the Beatitudes were untenable paradoxes for anyone who looked toward a material kingdom.[1] Thus Christ took His rightful place in the line of hope that ran through the Old Testament and brought it to its perfect development. Our Lord presented the spiritual kingdom of God under a twofold aspect, as *present* on this earth, developing with time, and also as *eschatological*, heavenly, and existing beyond the grave.[2]

2. The Present Kingdom of God

In His first sermons, our Lord began by taking up again the theme emphasized by John the Baptist and the later prophets: "The kingdom of God is at hand" (Mark 1:15, Matt. 4:17). But soon He made a transition, for in commenting at Nazareth on the passage from Isaias: "The Spirit of the Lord is upon me because he has anointed me; to bring good news to the poor he has sent me," He proclaimed: "Today this scripture has been fulfilled in your hearing" (Luke 4:18, 21). From then on, He would an-

[1] According to the Messianic ideas of the Old Testament, the Beatitudes should have been as follows: "Blessed are the valiant warriors. Blessed are the skillful politicians, etc." (For the Jews the word "blessed" had Messianic overtones and was particularly applicable to those who would have the good fortune to be alive at the time of the Messias.) But in contrast, Christ proclaimed: "Blessed are the poor, the pure of heart, and those who suffer. . . ."

[2] The expression which we translate as "the kingdom of God" really has two meanings, since it can be taken equally to mean "reign" or "kingdom of God." The Synoptic authors obviously use it in both senses; at one time they employ it to describe an organized, hierarchical kingdom, at another time to depict an interior invisible reign over men's hearts. St. Matthew, in order to avoid using the divine name, speaks of the kingdom "of heaven."

nounce: ". . . The kingdom of God has come upon you" (Matt. 12:28, Luke 11:20), and ". . . The kingdom of God is within you" (Luke 17:20).

But this kingdom was not established in its perfection all at once. It was indeed begun but it had to grow and develop. The majority of the parables of the kingdom stress this point—the parable of the seed in the earth (Mark 4:26), the grain of mustard seed (Matt. 13:31, Mark 4:30f., Luke 13:18f.), and the leaven in the dough (Matt. 13:33, Luke 13:20).

Furthermore, the present condition of the kingdom almost necessarily implies a state of imperfection. The best and the worst live side by side in it, as we learn from the parables of the weeds mixed with the good grain (Matt. 13:24f.), and the net that contains good and bad fish (Matt. 13:47f.). Christ warns us that these very different elements will remain mixed together for as long as the earthly phase of the kingdom will continue. Only at the "consummation of the world" will the definitive separation of the good and the bad take place. Thus the present, temporal kingdom will reach its normal fulfillment only in the eschatological kingdom at the end of time.

3. The Eschatological Kingdom of God

The perfect kingdom or reign, which is to begin at the end of time, is described in various images. The evangelists compare it to an eternal feast at which the elect will rejoice in the company of the holy patriarchs (Matt. 8:11, Luke 13:29); they will then appear as bright as the sun (Matt. 13:43), and will live like the angels of God (Matt. 22:30).

Yet, while this definitive kingdom will be the fruition

and fulfillment of the kingdom that was begun on earth, apparently it will not be established without an upheaval and a great change. It is a pre-existing kingdom, prepared for the elect from the creation of the world (Matt. 25:34), and it will, as it were, replace the present kingdom. Its establishment will be marked by the *parousia*,[3] the return of the Son of Man, who will come in power and glory to judge the world (Matt. 25:31f., Mark 13:26, Luke 21:25f.).

The time of our Lord's second coming is uncertain. If some texts are taken literally, the coming can be regarded as quite near (Matt. 16:28, Mark 9:1, Luke 9:27). But no one really knows the moment chosen by God (Matt. 24:36, Mark 13:32). That is why we must watch and be ready, with girded loins and lamps burning in our hands, as we are warned in the parables of the master's return (Luke 12:35f.) and the ten virgins (Luke 21:34f.).

The new kingdom will be that of the risen elect because the second coming of Christ will be accompanied by the resurrection of the body (Matt. 22:23f., Mark 12:18f., Luke 20:27f.). All this shows clearly enough that the idea of the eschatological kingdom follows the apocalyptic tradition.

The collective and social character of the kingdom is strongly underlined. The very expressions "kingdom of God," "kingdom of heaven," preclude putting the main emphasis on strictly individual happiness, and in both the

[3] The word *parousia* means "presence," "coming," or "arrival." In the New Testament it has assumed the technical sense of Christ's glorious return at the end of time, which is really the only sense in which it is now employed.

Old and New Testaments the kingdom is depicted as a perfect, happy community ruled by God. But it goes without saying that each individual has his own place in this community and that each must become integrated into the community.

Man must desire and seek eternal life before everything else; he must prefer it above all and, if necessary, must sacrifice everything for it, even his eye or his hand (Matt. 18:8f., Mark 9:43f.). Eternal life seems to be linked with the second coming of Christ because it is then, at the moment of judgment, that men will truly come into possession of eternal life. Then Christ will gather together his elect, separating them from the damned and assigning them their place in heaven (Matt. 25:31f., Luke 14:13f.).

The eternal life toward which everyone must aspire is in fact nothing else than participation in the eschatological kingdom which Christ's second coming will inaugurate. This life is the possession of the kingdom: "Come, blessed of my Father, take possession of the kingdom prepared for you from the foundation of the world" (Matt. 25:34). Thus, in general, the happy life of the next world is associated with the idea of the end of time, with Christ's second coming. Nevertheless, several texts allude to participation in this happiness before the eschatological events; for example, the parable of Lazarus the beggar refers to "Abraham's bosom" as the resting place of the just before the Resurrection, and our Lord promised the good thief, "This day thou shalt be with me in paradise." Yet this state will apparently be transitory because, since eternal life means possession of the perfect kingdom, it is to be expected that that life will begin at the end of time. And the idea is in harmony with the mentality of the Jews, who apparently did not envision an eternity transcending time as we do but who viewed eternity as time prolonged to infinity (the "ages to come") and limited only at its beginning, which was to coincide with Christ's second coming when the "present age" had come to an end.[4]

The kingdom has been prepared by God and is a pure gift of His kindness, but it is also a reward and hence must be earned. Not all who wish can enter even the earthly kingdom, for there are certain conditions to be fulfilled, namely, the conditions proclaimed in the Sermon on the Mount. On the last day each man must render an account of his stewardship (see the parable of the talents in Matt. 25:14f., and that of the gold pieces in Luke 19:12f.). Although the communal aspect of the kingdom is stressed, personal commitment is necessary, because entry into the kingdom is the reward for personal merit (Matt. 5:12, 19:20f., Mark 10:21f., Luke 18:22f.). Hence while hope in a future life must be based on God's free disposition, made be-

---

[4] In his excellent book, *Christ and Time* (Philadelphia: Westminster Press), the Protestant theologian, O. Cullmann, says that our present concept of an eternity completely different from time probably came from the Greek philosophers and was unknown to the Jews and the New Testament authors, for whom eternity was simply time without end and for whom one term "aeon" (*aión*) expressed both time and eternity.

"Aeon" can mean any one of the following but always with a completely temporal significance:

1) the present age limited at its origin by creation and at its end by the end of the world;

2) the period preceding creation, which is unlimited when viewed as extending into the past; this could be called an eternity;

3) the period that will begin at the end of the world and which will have no end; this is the "aeon" to come, the future age. It will begin at the end of the present "aeon" and is the eternal life mentioned in the Gospels.

fore the beginning of the world, and also upon our Lord's formal promise, our expectancy cannot be a smug contentment or pure passivity. The kingdom must, in a sense, be conquered: it must be merited personally.

4. The Object of Christian Hope

Christ came to perfect the hope expressed in the Old Testament, a hope fixed on the coming of the Messianic era. But the Jews' conception of the kingdom which was to be inaugurated by the Messias had to be corrected, or rather, it had to be freed of its material wrappings. To that task our Lord applied Himself by preaching in effect, "I am the Messias and I have come to establish the kingdom you are awaiting. It has already begun; it is among you; but make no mistake, it is a spiritual kingdom, one that holds sway in hearts. Yet it is also an organized kingdom with a hierarchy—Peter and the apostles—and with its own laws and sacraments; in a word, it is the Church. It will develop and cover the earth but will not reach perfection until the last day, at the second coming of the Son of Man and His return to glory. Then will be established the real kingdom of which the present one is only the seed and the preparation. Hence your hopes are not fulfilled by the coming of the Messias and the founding of the kingdom. Instead you must now look forward with even more eagerness to the perfection of the kingdom in eternity."

That is the new hope, Christian hope, that must replace the expectancy of the Jews. The object of this new hope is not the restoration of the Messianic kingdom, which is already in existence, but rather the fullness of this kingdom. And this fulfillment of the divine design, this final flowering of the kingdom, will be marked by a specific event, the second coming of Christ. Thus all the aspirations of God's new chosen race should reach out toward the return of the Lord, and all their hopes should be fixed thereon.

In addition to this, the main object of Christian hope, there are other objects which can be called minor and which our Lord proposed expressly in relation to the principal object. First, there is that material support which God assures to His faithful children, none of whom shall lack the necessities of life:

> Consider the ravens: they neither sow nor reap, they have neither storeroom nor barn; yet God feeds them. . . . Consider how the lilies grow; they neither toil nor spin, yet I say to you that not even Solomon in all his glory was arrayed like one of these (Luke 12:24, 27).

All our efforts should be bent toward the kingdom, and God will add everything else—material support and even earthly joys—without our having to worry about such things. Moreover, Christ promised to give His Church His unfailing aid during the whole existence of the present world (Matt. 28:20). Finally, we have been promised a gift which can scarcely be called minor, for it plays a very important role in the life of the present kingdom, namely, the gift of the Holy Ghost. We can look with absolute confidence to our Heavenly Father for the help of the Holy Spirit, particularly in times of persecution (Matt. 10:19, Mark 13:11, Luke 11:13, 12:11). He will give us the strength to bear witness to the Gospel. While St. Matthew's Gospel ends with Christ's promise of assistance, St. Luke's concludes with the announcement of the gift of the Holy Spirit. And the Acts of the Apostles especially show the place which the Holy Spirit occupied in the life of the early Church, truly replacing Christ after His Ascension and manifestly presiding over the Church, the Kingdom of God on earth.

ST. PAUL

1. Faith Is the Basis of Hope

In St. Paul's eyes, faith is the necessary foundation of hope. By its very nature, hope requires faith as its beginning, for it can exist only in relation to a good which is not yet possessed, which is not yet seen, and which therefore must first be an object of faith. Then, too, it is the imperfect nature of faith, which is actually knowledge without sight, that allows hope to exist and gives birth to it: "For in hope were we saved. But hope that is seen is not hope. For how can a man hope for what he sees?" (Rom. 8:24).

The Epistle to the Hebrews sums up the relationship of faith and hope in a terse formula that expresses well the unity between them: "Faith is the substance of things to be hoped for . . ." (Heb. 11:1). According to the Epistle to the Romans, the example of Abraham is the classic illustration of hope, for faith and hope were so united in him that he is the model of all believers:

> Abraham hoping against hope believed, so that he became the father of many nations, according to what was said, "So shall thy offspring be." And without weakening in faith, he considered his own deadened body (for he was almost a hundred years old) and the deadened womb of Sara; and yet in

view of the promise of God, he did not waver through un-
belief but was strengthened in faith, giving glory to God,
being fully aware that whatever God has promised He is
able also to perform (Rom. 4:18–21).

2. The Object of Hope: the Glory of God

a) For St. Paul hope is a specifically Christian virtue just
as faith and charity are. Christians have a true vocation to
hope (Eph. 1:18) and their common hope is also a sign
and an element of their unity:

> I therefore, the prisoner in the Lord, exhort you to walk in
> a manner worthy of the calling with which you were called,
> with all humility and meekness, with patience, bearing with
> one another in love, careful to preserve the unity of the Spirit
> in the bond of peace: one body and one Spirit, even as you
> were called in one hope of your calling; one Lord, one faith,
> one baptism; one God and Father of all, who is above all, and
> throughout all, and in us all (Eph. 4:1–6).

Hence true hope is a Christian privilege, as St. Paul
reminded the Ephesians:

"Bear in mind that once you . . . were . . . without
Christ, excluded as aliens from the community of Israel,
and strangers to the covenants of the promise, having no
hope, and without God in the world" (Eph. 2:11–12). And
when speaking to the Thessalonians about the fate of the
dead, he declared:

"But we would not, brethren, have you ignorant concerning those who are asleep, lest you should grieve, even
as others who have no hope" (1 Thess. 4:13). Like faith,
hope is a characteristic of the present state of the Christian.
All the gifts, all the charisms will pass away, but charity

will always remain: "So there abide faith, hope and charity; but the greatest of these is charity" (1 Cor. 13:13).

b) What is the precise object of Christian hope? We must remember that hope is not focused only on this life: "If with this life only in view we have had hope in Christ, we are of all men, the most to be pitied" (1 Cor. 15:19).

In specifying the object of hope, St. Paul generally uses three terms—salvation (Rom. 13:11, 1 Thess. 5:8, 2 Cor. 1:6f.), eternal life (Rom. 6:22, Tit. 1:2), and glory—but he shows a marked preference for the third term, glory. Actually all three mean the same thing, but St. Paul seems to consider that the word "glory" exactly defines the object of hope.

Basically, it is God's glory that we must await and hope for: "Having been justified therefore by faith, let us have peace with God through our Lord Jesus Christ, through whom we also have access by faith unto that grace in which we stand, and exult in the hope of the glory of the sons of Christ" (Rom. 5:1–2). "For the grace of God our Savior has appeared to all men, instructing us, in order that, rejecting ungodliness and worldly lusts, we may live temperately and justly and piously in this world; looking for the blessed hope and glorious coming of our great God and Savior, Jesus Christ" (Tit. 2:11–13).

But God's glory is also ours in the sense that God manifests His glory in us, for we shall share the full glory of Christ:

Therefore if you have risen with Christ, seek the things that are above, where Christ is seated at the right hand of God. Mind the things that are above, not the things that are

on earth. For you have died, and your life is hidden with
Christ in God. When Christ, your life, shall appear, then you
too will appear with Him in glory (Col. 3:1–4).

. . . Even we, all of us, once led our lives in the desires of
our flesh, doing the promptings of our flesh and of our
thoughts, and were by nature children of wrath even as the
rest. But God, who is rich in mercy, by reason of his very
great love wherewith he has loved us even when we were
dead by reason of our sins, brought us to life together with
Christ (by grace you have been saved), and raised us up together, and seated us together in heaven in Christ Jesus . . .
(Eph. 2:3–7;[5] see also Rom. 8:17, 2 Thess. 2:13).

This glory which we are called to share will not be in
us a passing glory, like the fleeting reflection which Moses
carried on his countenance after he had talked with
Yahweh. On the contrary, it will be an essentially divine
glory, permanent and immortal, for it truly is eternal life
(Rom. 2:7f., 2 Cor. 3:7–18). St. Paul multiplies terms in
trying to define it; he says that it will be "the revelation of
the sons of God," "the freedom of the glory of the sons
of God," "the adoption as sons" (Rom. 8:19–23).

Now this, the object of our hope—glory, eternal life,
salvation—is the heritage which God promised to Abraham.
And because the idea of this heritage was transmitted under
the form of the kingdom, the Synoptic authors write about
the *kingdom of God*. That is also the reason why St. Paul,
using parallel and synonymous expressions, speaks of inheriting everlasting life (Tit. 3:7), or of inheriting glory
(Eph. 1:14, 1:18) or, most often, of inheriting the king-

[5] It is worth noting that St. Paul here speaks of the eschatological bene-
fits as past whereas in other places, e.g., in the Epistle to the Romans, he
refers to them as future. This is a characteristic of the Epistles of the
captivity, of which the Epistle to the Ephesians is one.

dom of God (1 Cor. 6:9–10, Gal. 5:21, Eph. 5:5, etc.).
We even find that he uses in the same sentence two phrases
that are obviously identical in meaning—inheriting the kingdom of God and inheriting incorruptibility (1 Cor. 15:50).
Thus there is no doubt that for him, glory, salvation, eternal life, and the kingdom of God are simply different names
for the one thing, the object of the Promise.

c) For St. Paul, the kingdom of God is clearly eschatological, as is evidenced by the way he equates it with incorruptibility and eternal glory. Sometimes he even expressly calls it the "*heavenly* kingdom" of God (2 Tim.
4:18), thus linking it with the end of time and the second
coming of Christ. This return of our Lord, a specific, concrete event, dominates the whole field of hope and gathers
together in itself all the elements of the object of hope,
for Christ's return will mark the establishment of the kingdom and the full realization of the Promise.

Our Lord's second coming is also presented as the
clearly defined object of our expectancy under the different terms which the Apostle uses to describe it; most often
it is "the coming of our Lord Jesus Christ" or "the day of
the Lord," while sometimes he calls it "the appearance of
our Lord Jesus Christ," or "the revelation of the Lord
Jesus" (see 1 Cor. 1:7, 2 Thess. 1:7, Phil. 3:20, Tit. 2:13,
Heb. 9:28, etc.). Confirming this idea, St. Peter in his
Second Epistle not only lays stress on awaiting the day of
the Lord but also speaks of the faithful as those who
"hasten toward" its coming (2 Pet. 3:12). The reason is
that, in apostolic times, the Christians thought that Christ's
second coming was imminent, so much so that St. Paul
felt obliged to put the Thessalonians on their guard, and St.

Peter felt he had to justify the delay in the fulfillment of the Promise by attributing it to God's patience and to His allowing a period for repentance (1 Thess. 5:1–12, 2 Thess. 2:1–12, 2 Pet. 3).

St. Paul loves to describe all the events surrounding Christ's second coming[6]—the precursory signs, the general resurrection, Christ's appearance in majesty, the last judgment, and finally the end of the world. It would be beside the point here for us to pause to examine these descriptions since we are concerned with the second coming only as the object of Christian hope. The general resurrection, for which there is abundant proof (see 1 Cor. 15 especially), is a condition for entry into the eternal kingdom because it will be, at least for the elect, the beginning of an eternal union with Christ (1 Cor. 15, 1 Thess. 4:16–17), and of a state in which the body will be incorruptible, glorious, spiritual and full of strength (1 Cor. 15:35–55). In contrast, St. Paul apparently did not concern himself about the fate of souls before the general resurrection. In fact, he scarcely mentions them, and when he does, he calls them simply "they who have fallen asleep" (1 Cor. 15:15–20, cf. 1 Thess. 4:13–15). This omission is easily explained by two reasons related to the concept of hope. First, if the second coming was near, as the early Christian apparently thought, the transitory state of the dead was only of very limited importance; and secondly, in the ordinary perspective of Scripture, the future of the individual is neither separate nor separable from the fate of God's people as such, from the salvation of all, with which the Scriptures are mainly concerned.

[6] See L. Cerfaux, *Christ in the Theology of Saint Paul*. Herder, 1959.

Finally, the end of the world will come after Christ has pronounced judgment. The Savior's return will be His definitive victory over all His enemies, for, having triumphed over sin and over the prince of this world, He will have to overcome only the old adversary, death, and this He will do on the last day. Then His work as Savior will be done and He will be able to place the kingdom, and dominion over all things, in His Father's hands (1 Cor. 15:24–28). This will be the end of this "age," the end of the present world, and also, as St. Peter says, the beginning of another world, of "new heavens and a new earth" (see 1 Cor. 1:8, 2 Cor. 1:13–14; 2 Pet. 3:10f.).

Hence Christ's return is, in actuality, the end and object of Christian hope because it will bring with it all the things which that hope awaits. Christian hope, therefore, has two main characteristics:

First, it is centered on a fact, on a historical event that will take place on a definite day in the course of time. That is why hope very naturally includes a reaching forward in desire toward this future event. Because of this reaching out to an ensured future, hope is the great support of Christian action, the source of patience and courage in the trials of life. The hopeful man is like the runner who keeps his eyes fixed on the end of the course and the victor's crown (see Rom. 5:3, 8:17f., 1 Cor. 9:24–27, 2 Cor. 4:16–18).

Secondly, the object of Christian hope is something that essentially interests God's people as a whole. The expectation of attaining a good that is formally individual and that has no express relationship with the Christian community is not part of Christian hope and occurs nowhere in the Bible. And for St. Paul, salvation is not merely the salvation of all God's people but a cosmic salvation, since all creation awaits deliverance "groan[ing] and travail-[ing]," tormented by its desire for the day when it, too, will find its state of glory (cf. Rom. 8:19–22).

3. Through Hope We Already Possess the Goods of Eternity

There remains one important detail about the functioning of hope. The object of hope, which, by definition, is attainable only in the future, is nevertheless already present in a mysterious way. We must not think that hope must needs give us an exclusively eschatological outlook as if the central event of the story of salvation were still to come. That event has already happened: Christ has won salvation for us. But Christ's first coming reaches out over the centuries, as it were, to His second coming as to the crowning of the work of salvation which He has already fully accomplished and which comes to men in the life of the Church.

Hope gives us something of our future glory, even in our present state, for it allows us to rejoice, even now, in the certitude of that future glory, since we know that our hope is assured and that it cannot deceive us (Rom. 5:1–5). Hence the general principle that, through hope, we possess the goods of eternity imperfectly but nonetheless really. It is thus that we now share in God's glory. We know that in heaven we shall see Him face to face, but we see Him even now although only as through a mirror (1 Cor. 13:12). We are mirrors of divine glory and we are called to make ourselves completely in the image that we reflect (2 Cor. 3:14–18).[7] Above all, we now possess salvation through the

[7] On this point, see L. Cerfaux, *op. cit.*

grace of Christ, and salvation is the anticipated possession of eternal life, "for in hope were we saved" (see Rom. 8:24, 5:17f.). It would be hard to emphasize sufficiently the tone of present reality in this phrase. Although the consummation of our salvation is still to come, we now possess our salvation in hope. We have been saved by Christ and we need only to cooperate with His grace to taste the fruits of redemption. We shall not savor the first fruits of salvation until the resurrection of the body; yet, while we wait to be fully conformed to the risen Christ, we can, in a real sense, enter the life of the resurrection and put on the risen Christ (see Rom. 6:3f.).

This anticipated possession of the object of hope makes the last things themselves present so that the eschatological era has already begun. The sure sign of this is the gift of the Holy Spirit which we have received, for the Holy Spirit is the guarantee, the pledge, and the first fruits of our future heritage—full and definitive redemption (Rom. 8:23, 2 Cor. 1:22, 5:5, Eph. 1:13). And St. Peter in his sermon on Pentecost showed that the widespread gift of the Spirit is the sign of the last days announced by Joel (Acts 2:16ff.). That is the new, the Christian concept of time: with Christ we have entered a new era, and the world to come, the future eternal world, is already here.[8]

8 With O. Cullmann (*op. cit.*) we must note that here we are really dealing with a new, twofold division of time centered on Christ (time before Christ and time after Christ). This twofold division can be superimposed on the old threefold division (the triple *aión*) without destroying it. The signs of the future age, of the last days, are already here, but the presence of sin, which is one of the signs of the era before the second coming, still remains. In possessing Christ, we already possess the essentials, salvation and eternal life; yet the second coming is still the event that is to mark the definitive transformation of the kingdom.

4. Christ, Our Hope

For St. Paul, Christian hope is undoubtedly based upon
the Promise, or more precisely, both on the Promise made
by God in the beginning and on God's absolute fidelity to
His word: "Let us hold fast the confession of our hope
without wavering, for he who has given the promise is faithful" (Heb. 10:23, see also 1 Cor. 1:9, 1 Thess. 5:24, 2 Tim.
2:13, Tit. 1:2, Heb. 6:13–20). We must link this idea to
one of the great themes of St. Paul's doctrine. After the
rejection of the Jews, the Christian community, that is,
the Church, became the true people of God, the Israel of
God. Hence the Church has taken the place of the people
of the Old Testament and inherits all their privileges. Now
the promise which God made to Abraham and his descendants, the inheritance promised to the patriarch, is one of
the most important of these privileges. St. Paul under-
stands the initial promise in a sense which goes far beyond
the history of the people of the Old Law, and he teaches
that Christ is the heir to whom the inheritance was promised (Rom. 4:12–16, Gal. 3:15–22). That is why the glory
and the eternal life that come to us through Christ are
the true heritage, the real object of the initial promise, and
are to be identified with the kingdom of God.

The strength of the promise as a motive for hope is con-
firmed by the fact that we already have the first pledges
that it is being kept. God's promise has already begun
to produce its fruits, for we now have salvation by grace
and hence the assurance of future glory—all of which come
to us from Christ and from Him alone. It is from Him that
we expect to receive everything that we await and hope

for. It is He who saves us and gives us a new life; it was He who arose from the dead as a pledge of our resurrection; and it is He who is the mediator of the new covenant (see Rom. 5, and Heb. 9). Therefore, Christ is the great support of our hope, or as St. Paul calls Him simply, "Christ Jesus, our hope" (1 Tim. 1:1), and this applies especially to the risen Christ.

The promise which God made and which Christ fulfilled is part of that divine plan, that mysterious design hidden from the beginning of time by which God, in His wisdom and goodness, has arranged everything for His elect and which was revealed only at the appointed time. Thus from the start we find God's free arrangements and His sovereign, gratuitous design (Eph. 1:3–12).

All of this is basis enough for our hope which, however, still requires us to play an active and efficacious role. Everything has been prepared for us, Christ has won salvation for us, but still we must enter into God's plans and become one with Christ. If we are to share in His glory, we must become like Him in His life and sufferings.

5. Hope Sustains the Christian's Whole Life

We scarcely need to emphasize anew the important role which hope should play in the Christian life. Let us simply recall that St. Paul habitually mentions it in the same breath with faith and charity, with which it forms a trilogy that must characterize the Christian life in the present age (1 Cor. 13:13, Col. 1:5, 1 Thess. 1:3, 5:8, Heb. 10:22ff.).

In St. Paul, as in the Synoptics, hope is completely orientated toward the Second Coming, which will manifest God's glory in us. As we have seen, we already possess the seeds of this glory, whence comes that "assurance" which hope gives to Christians and upon which St. Paul insists so much, that certitude that everything in our lives works for the glory of God.

Even our very sufferings and trials are pledges of the reality of our hope and are a source of the assurance we have just mentioned, for everything is in labor to bring forth future glory in us, in our bodies in expectation of the resurrection, and in the whole of creation, which groans for liberation. And the Holy Spirit Himself, who has been given to us as a pledge, joins His ineffable groanings in us to those of the universe.

The Epistle of the Romans contains one of the most beautiful passages ever written on hope. It is a passage upon which everyone who feels overwhelmed by trials should meditate:

> The Spirit himself gives testimony to our spirit that we are sons of God. But if we are sons, we are heirs also: heirs indeed of God and joint heirs with Christ, provided, however, we suffer with him that we may also be glorified with him. For I reckon that the sufferings of the present time are not worthy to be compared with the glory to come that will be revealed in us. For the eager longing of creation awaits the revelation of the sons of God. For creation was made subject to vanity—not by its own will but by reason of him who made it subject—in hope, because creation itself also will be delivered from its slavery to corruption into the freedom of the glory of the sons of God. For we know that all creation groans and travails in pain until now. And not only it, but we ourselves also who have the first fruits of the Spirit— we ourselves groan within ourselves, waiting for the adoption as sons, the redemption of our body. For in hope were we saved. But hope that is seen is not hope. For how can a man

hope for what he sees? But if we hope for what we do not see, we wait for it with patience. But in like manner the Spirit also helps our weakness. For we do not know what we should pray for as we ought, but the Spirit himself pleads for us with unutterable groanings. And he who searches the hearts knows what the Spirit desires, that he pleads for the saints according to God (Rom. 8:16–27).

St. Paul's words to the Corinthians are no less fervent and touching:

. . . We do not lose heart. On the contrary, even though our outer man is decaying, yet our inner man is being re-newed day by day. For our present light affliction, which is for the moment, prepares for us an eternal weight of glory that is beyond all measure; while we look not at the things that are seen, but at the things that are not seen. For the things that are seen are temporal, but the things that are not seen are eternal. For we know that if the earthly house in which we dwell be destroyed, we have a building from God, a house not made by human hands, eternal in the heavens. And indeed, in the present state we groan, yearning to be clothed over with that dwelling of ours which is from heaven if in-deed we shall be found clothed and not naked. For we who are in this tent sigh under our burden because we do not wish to be unclothed, but rather clothed over, that what is mortal may be swallowed up by life. Now he who made us for this very thing is God, who has given us the Spirit as its pledge. Always full of courage, then, and knowing that while we are in the body we are exiled from the Lord—for we walk by faith and not by sight—we even have the courage to prefer to be exiled from the body and be at home with the Lord (2 Cor. 4:16–5:8).

ST. JOHN

In all of his writings, St. John scarcely mentions hope, and when he does he tells us nothing new about it. Yet more than any other sacred writer, more even than St. Paul himself, he stresses the profound unity that exists between the life which Christ gives us now and the eternal life which shall be begun by the resurrection. He constantly uses such expressions as: "He who believes in the son *has* everlasting life" (John 3:36); "He who eats my flesh and drinks my blood *has* everlasting life and I will raise him up on the last day" (John 6:55); "He who hears my words . . . *has* life everlasting, and does not come to judgment, but *has passed* from death to life" (John 5:24); "He who believes in me *has* life everlasting" (John 6:47). Obviously for him eternal life has already begun and with Christ we have entered "the age to come."

But it is in the Apocalypse that, without using the word itself, St. John gives us the most beautiful and vivid illustration of hope. Here he describes the battles that await the Church, the assaults of all the enemies of Christ and the enemies of the very name "Christian," and he concludes with the triumph of the Lamb in which all those who have persevered to the end shall take part. The whole history of the Church, which appears so utterly tragic in this dramatic summary, leads to this final glorification, so that the Apocalypse can be summed up by saying that the unloosed forces of evil cannot prevail against the Church's constant, unwavering expectancy of the coming of Christ's kingdom and His final triumph at the appointed time. All the immense aspiration of Christian peoples will be fulfilled by the appearance of a new heaven, a new earth, and a new Jerusalem, adorned like a bride for her spouse. Then hope will have finished its course; it will have attained its object. Then it can dissolve into complete joy:

> And I heard a loud voice from the throne saying, "Behold the dwelling of God with men, and he will dwell with them. And they will be his people, and God himself will be with them as their God. And God will wipe away every tear from their eyes. And death shall be no more; neither shall there be mourning, nor crying, nor pain any more, for the former things have passed away" (Apoc. 21:3–4).

The Apocalypse closes with an express call for the Lord's return: "And the Spirit and the bride say, 'Come!' And let him who hears say, 'Come!' And let him who thirsts come; and he who wishes, let him receive the water of life freely . . . Amen! Come, Lord Jesus!"

Thus at the end the prophets of the Old Testament, St. Paul, and the evangelists all join in the same cry of impatience and expectancy, in the great call of hope: "*Maranatha!* Come, Lord!"

··⊰[4]⊱··

From Revelation to Theology

✠

AN EVIDENT DECLINE

If we go directly from making a study of hope in Scripture to a modern theological treatise, or, which is almost the same thing, to the teachings of the great doctors of the Middle Ages, we shall note a marked change in perspective.

According to Scripture, hope is a journey in absolute confidence, based on the divine promise, toward the kingdom of God. The New Testament depicts this kingdom as already begun but still imperfect in its present stage, destined to grow and to be transformed into a perfect, eternal kingdom at the end of time. As we saw, in Scripture hope is centered on a specific event, namely, the Second Coming of Christ with its glorious consequences, the general resurrection and entry into the perfected kingdom.

Now, when we turn to a theological treatise on hope, we find that eternal happiness, the possession of God, is presented as the object and final end of the virtue. We can hardly fail to be surprised at such a change of viewpoint, and we are immediately struck by the substitution of an abstract term for a whole complex of specific and vivid ideas, and by the substitution of the bare phrase "eternal happiness" for the detailed description of the glorious kingdom found in the New Testament.

Here we touch upon the profound difference between revelation and theology. Revelation is not professedly "metaphysical," but is simply God's setting forth to men "the mystery of salvation" in terms which they can understand, which yet must serve to explain the unexplainable. Moreover, while the revelation of the mystery is destined for all men, it is nevertheless proposed to them through the mediation of a specific people belonging to a definite race and distinguished by certain ethnological, cultural, and historical characteristics. Therefore revelation took place in concrete human circumstances. But theology is research and reflection performed by enlightened minds on the object revealed. And since by its very nature the mind must try to understand and reason, and since it seeks logic and unity in everything, it examines and dissects the object revealed in order to discern the "intelligible values" contained therein.

Consequently theology must endeavor to find in the object of hope the essential principle around which all the elements of hope are arranged. And theology finds this principle in the real, personal possession of God Himself in a face-to-face vision which it considers the basic underlying feature of the biblical images of the kingdom. In this, theology takes its stand on the only texts that raise a corner of the veil from the life beyond: "We see now through a mirror in an obscure manner, but then face to face. Now I know in part, but then I shall know even as I have been known" (1 Cor. 13:12). "Now we are the children of God, and it has not yet appeared what we shall be. We know that, when he appears, we shall be like to him, for we shall see him just as he is" (1 John 3:2).

It is this supreme act of perfect union with God that constitutes man's happiness. Hence although the vocabulary and perhaps the emphasis of theology differ from those of revelation, just as the nature and methods of each are not the same, there is no real divergence between the two, and the evolution which we have pointed out here is quite normal.

Nevertheless, we can still ask whether theology has not tended to overemphasize the necessary distinction between it and revelation as a result of circumstances and certain historical conditions. Theology may have been formed and developed as a metaphysical science, as an intellectual discipline rather than a doctrine of salvation, but, be that as it may, the case of hope, at least, appears quite characteristic in this respect.

THE "ACT OF HOPE"

Let us take the "act" of hope as Catholics say [1] it or make it interiorly: "O my God, I firmly hope to receive from

[1] How paradoxical it is to speak of *saying* an *act*!

you, through the merits of Jesus Christ, heaven and all the graces necessary to merit it, because you are infinitely good, omnipotent, and faithful to your promises." We must not forget that no formula is perfect. This one has the advantage of presenting a synthesis of all the classical theological elements of an act of hope—the special nature of the act ("I firmly hope . . ."), the principal and secondary material objects of the act, that is, the things hoped for ("heaven and all the graces necessary to merit it"), and finally the formal object or basis of the act (the merits of Christ, and God's goodness, omnipotence, and fidelity.) [2]

But we must properly understand this little theological synthesis and not empty the act of hope of its essential dynamism. When you ask them, many sincere Christians will tell you that this act simply means: "O God, You're so good that I believe I'll go to heaven when you call me—but, of course, I'm in no hurry to get there!"

First of all, we must note the relationship between faith and hope, and the practical difficulty of always distinguishing properly between them. Actually, hope is not belief, which belongs essentially to the order of knowledge, but is rather a reaching out of the will toward a good to be possessed. Furthermore, the conviction characteristic of belief is likely to seem a kind of tranquil possession or else sheer optimism, without fear as well as without great vigor. How far removed this is from the expectancy, the waiting, which we find in the Scriptures, and which is so full of assurance yet also of pulsating impatience and restless fervor! How far it is from that supernatural verve which gives the whole of life an impetus that nothing can stop!

[2] Later we shall speak more at length about this double object.

Again, the object thus proposed is *"my* salvation," *"my* eternal happiness," with all that is needed to attain thereto. That is fair enough, but such emphasis on individualism (*"my* salvation") is very different from the emphasis of Scripture, where we find all the people of God and even all creation reaching out toward the manifestation of God's glory in the second coming of Christ. When one tries to tell the faithful today that the precise object of hope is Christ's return, the *parousia*, they are completely flabbergasted. Therefore there are certain biblical dimensions which we must restore to hope.

TWO DIMENSIONS TO BE RESTORED

1. "Horizontal" and "Vertical" Hope

We have seen how, in the New Testament, hope was turned toward an *event*, a specific fact which summed up all the expectancy of God's people. Thus hope had a well-marked target. Then, too, time played an important role in hope, which carried the Christian across the unfolding of temporal events to a definite day and moment. To use Gabriel Marcel's beautiful expression, hope then truly seemed like a vista through time. It is true that the kingdom which it awaited was really a transcendent and preexisting one; yet this kingdom was to be fully realized only at the end of time, at the end of this present "age" or *aión.* Hence came the real reaching out toward the end of time which characterized scriptural hope, or, as we call it here, *"horizontal"* hope.

This characteristic does not appear very clearly in our

usual concept of hope, and the eschatological aspect of the virtue has mostly been omitted from our treatises on the subject. We are told instead that the object of hope is the possession of God, who is our happiness. Therefore it is scarcely too much to say that the object of the virtue has been despoiled and reduced, taken out of the temporal movement of hope and regarded in a completely metaphysical light. Undoubtedly, hope still retains all its riches for the philosopher and it is still turned to the future since it lasts while the possession of eternal bliss is deferred. Yet the movement of hope is no longer "horizontal" but "vertical" in the sense that its object is now less a future event than a metaphysical aim which exists here and now and with which we can immediately come in contact by a theological act of hope, not an act which essentially traverses time but which basically transcends the natural order. Hence there is reason to fear that hope may keep the Christian soul in a pleasant tranquility and an assurance which tends to render it inactive and less careful about being vigilant and prepared to meet trials with the confidence that it will eventually overcome them all. Only too often hope is in danger of being reduced to a kind of bland and lazy certitude, to a conviction that we will gain paradise when the time comes, which time, of course, will be deferred as long as possible! Therefore we could also call this type of hope "static" as opposed to "dynamic."

2. Community and Individual Hope

When Scripture speaks of the kingdom, it insists on the communal aspect of the object of hope, and in its pages eternal life, even under the aspect of a reward for personal acts, is viewed in close connection with the community—the individual Christian will be reunited with Christ and all the elect on the day of judgment and will live with Him in His eternal kingdom. Thus the Christian does not realize his destiny alone but rather enters into the possession of his heritage with all the people of God.

However, once we isolate the vision of the divine essence, which is an eminently personal and individual act, as the essential reality of eternal life, then the communal aspect of the beatific vision is inevitably reduced to a secondary place. Then we place alongside the principal object a series of "additions" to eternal happiness, such as the society of the elect, the sight of the risen Christ, or the resurrection of our own bodies. Consequently we tend to leave out of account the close bonds of kinship which the Christian has with the great divine family in times of trial as well as in eternal glory.

As is obvious, we have presented here an extremely simplified description of the distorted view which those who are familiar with the Bible alone will receive from modern manuals of theology.

···⊰[5]⊱···

Development of the Doctrine of Hope

✠

Hope, as such, was certainly not a major subject of theoretical study among the first Christian thinkers or the Fathers of the Church.[1] Even St. Augustine, who usually wrote at such length, devoted to hope only a few of the one hundred and nineteen chapters in his *Enchiridion de fide, spe, et caritate.* Nevertheless, one of the most debated problems in the early Church was the object of hope, that is, the *parousia*, especially the time it would occur, and the concept of the eschatological kingdom.[2]

[1] See Tixeront, *Histoire des dogmes dans l'antiquité chrétienne* (Paris: Gabalda), and R. Draguet, *Histoire du dogme catholique* (Paris: Albin Michel, 1941), from whom we borrow these notes.

[2] Since it is impossible to study the whole historical evolution of a doctrine in a book as short as this, we shall limit ourselves to describing the principal stages in the development of this particular point. Later we shall deal briefly with the diverse positions of Jansenism and Quietism regarding the connections between hope and love.

The primitive community made the return of Christ the precise object of its expectation and linked eternal life to the *parousia*, as is expressly stated in the *Didaché*. But as time went by and the *parousia* did not occur, the problem of the state of souls between death and the general resurrection assumed great importance. Yet, the idea of an imminent *parousia* and of its close connection with the fullness of eternal life was so fixed in the minds of the early Christians that several centuries were to pass before an answer was given to the question of the soul's beatitude immediately after death. Leaving aside the Gnostics, Marcionists, and Docetists, who denied the *parousia* and the resurrection of the body, we can distinguish in Christian tradition three main stages of development before the growth of theological systems in the Middle Ages.

MILLENARIANISM

This was a belief which evolved from the expectation of the *parousia*, especially in the second and third centuries. It can be summed up as follows: Christ is going to return in order to establish on earth a thousand-year kingdom in which the elect, after being raised from the dead, will participate. But this recompense of the elect will be only provisional, because the end of the world, the last judgment, and the definitive decree of reward or punishment, will take place at the end of the thousand years. This erroneous doctrine drew its strength from the ancient Jewish ideas of the temporal reign of the Messias, and claimed the support of certain passages in the Apocalypse. St. Irenaeus adopted it; it won over Egypt, and Tertullian spread it in Africa. Yet from the beginning, many Christians, among whom were Origen and his disciples, fought it strenuously. However, as time went on, it spread in ever-widening circles, for it served in times of crises as a kind of Utopian dream.

ORIGEN'S INFLUENCE

The second period in the development of the doctrine of hope is marked by Origen's name and influence. His teacher, Clement of Alexandria, the "Christian Gnostic," aroused his interest in eschatological problems. Origen taught that the future life consists in full revelation and full light. However, when the just die and before they are admitted to heaven, they pass through paradise, which is a subterranean region where they are purified by a baptism of fire. Those who have nothing to expiate pass through without suffering and then ascend from sphere to sphere, being purified more and more and receiving an increase of light until at last they are reunited with Christ. The body is raised from the dead in a new matter and in a perfect (*i.e.*, "spherical"!) form. Origen finally taught that the *apocatastasis* would occur, that is, that all intelligent creatures, even the damned and the devils after purification by fire, would in the end be restored to friendship with God. His theories, especially the *apocatastasis*, won over minds as great as that of St. Gregory of Nyssa, and his influence is found in the works of many of the other fathers of the Church.

Among the Latin fathers of the third and fourth centuries, there were many opinions on the state of souls after death. Most of them believed that the *parousia* was close at hand, and many thought that between death and the last judgment there is an intermediate state in which the elect have only a foretaste of heaven, and the damned, a foretaste of hell (*see* Tertullian and St. Hippolytus in the third century, and even later, St. Ambrose at the end of the fourth century). Some, such as St. Hilary, Zeno, St. Jerome, and St. Ambrose, held that neither the just nor the impious will be judged at the general judgment because their fate will already have been decided, and that only those sinners who have to be purified after death will then be examined. However, in 543, Pope Vigilius condemned Origenism, especially the theory of the "perfect" nature of risen bodies ("spherical" and "ethereal" bodies) and also the *apocatastasis*, thus indirectly affirming the eternity of hell. But Origen's authority was not completely supplanted until the appearance of St. Augustine, who, in his turn, dominated almost all theological thought until the Renaissance of the twelfth century, and whose influence was felt throughout the theology of the Middle Ages.

ST. AUGUSTINE

At first, St. Augustine accepted Millenarianism, but later he rejected it categorically and held instead that souls receive their reward or punishment immediately after death, although he did believe that this reward or punishment would be complete only after the general resurrection. Do the souls of the just see God while they are awaiting the resurrection? Augustine did not say so except in the case of the martyrs.

He also held that, at the resurrection, flesh will remain flesh and will not become spirit, but will be "spiritual flesh." He taught that the pain of hell will be eternal (thus every trace of Origenism is eliminated) and visualized a purification for certain sins (purgatory). He held that beatitude consists in the face-to-face vision of God, but he confessed that he was unable to decide whether or not the elect will see God with their bodily eyes.

The Greek fathers of the same era were less certain about the intuitive vision of God, and much later, even among the Latin writers, Pope John XXII voiced the opinion, which he retracted before his death, that the elect will have to wait for the general judgment to possess the vision of the divine essence. But in 1336, his successor, Benedict XII, defined the doctrine that the completely pure souls of the elect enjoy the immediate and face-to-face vision of the divine essence.

The doctrine of the intermediate state of purgatory developed slowly, based upon the "purifying fire" mentioned in Sacred Scripture and upon the ancient custom of suffrages for the dead. The dogma of purgatory was defined at the Council of Florence (1438) and reaffirmed at the Council of Trent (1545–1563).

THE SCHOLASTIC THEOLOGIANS

Our brief remarks so far are sufficient to show that the definition of the essential element in the object of hope was elaborated only after much thought. However, once the immediate possession of God by the souls of the just after death was established, the importance of the *parousia* began to wane, and the longing for the resurrection of the body became secondary because, once the beatific vision is attained, salvation is assured. In addition, the final glory of the Church, the kingdom of God, which was also included in the *parousia*, seems to have been eliminated almost entirely from the ambit of hope.

The latter development was due, at least partly, to a sentence of St. Augustine's which was to weigh heavily upon the doctrine of hope during the whole Middle Ages.[3] Actually, St. Augustine believed that hope could be focused only on a *personal* good; hence a communal hope would seem impossible, since each individual member of God's people (to which the inheritance was promised) can apparently hope for the glory of the Church only insofar as he finds therein his own personal happiness.

Furthermore, scholastic theology, being markedly metaphysical, was intent on searching out as far as possible the "necessary reasons" of everything, and this inevitably reduced an *event* (*i.e.*, a contingent fact) such as the *parousia* to a secondary place in the rational organization of the object of hope.

Fortunately, St. Thomas, while he re-adopted and defended Augustine's opinion, restored the communal aspect to the object of hope. In reality, although hope, when left to follow its own impetus, can desire only personal goods, the same is not true of hope nourished by charity, for

[3] *Cf.* P. Charles, *Spes Christi* in *Nouvelle Revue Théologique*, 1937, pp. 1057–1075.

charity identifies us with those whom we love; it causes us to desire their good as if it were our own, and therefore it allows us to hope as sincerely for the good of all those to whom we are joined by charity as for our own personal good. Perhaps it may be objected that this is introducing communal hope "by the back door," as it were. However, hope separated from charity is not perfect hope, that fullness of hope of which the New Testament speaks. But we must still investigate the role of Christ's second coming. We shall do so in the next chapter.

6

Theological Analysis

✠

HOPE, A THEOLOGICAL VIRTUE

1. The Theological Trilogy

The trilogy of the theological virtues, faith, hope and charity, is one of the foundations of Catholic theology and is the very mainspring of the Christian life. The theological virtues are distinguished from the moral virtues by the fact that they have God as their direct object. Through them we can truly live the divine life because they allow us to partake actively in the very life of God. They are, as it were, the faculties through which grace acts.

Because the theological virtues form this very special trilogy, we are accustomed to grouping them together and regarding them as a unit. It is only logical that we should do so, but we may perhaps be sacrificing too much by thus preferring a logical structure to a "living" one. The logical approach is incomparably better for teaching and scientific purposes, but if we are to respect the "living" structure of Christianity, we must study the theological virtues as part of the Christian life, as part of an organism that is born and develops.

As a result of keeping these three virtues together by stressing the fact that they all have the same object, namely, God apprehended directly, we run the risk of isolating them from the other virtues, thus breaking the internal unity of the Christian life. In addition, we are liable to forget that each of the theological virtues has very specific and completely distinct functions. Therefore, having asserted their theological character, we must next try to put them in their proper places in the organic structure of the Christian life in accordance with their functions. To do this fully would mean re-organizing the whole of moral theology. Here we can do no more than make a few short observations on the matter.

We enter the Christian life through faith, which is the essential condition for admission to God's people, to the kingdom. Faith is the basic acceptance of God's revelation of the mystery of salvation, a free, total acceptance, our complete response to God's call. And this acceptance of living faith will entail, as a normal consequence, the rest of the Christian life.

Living the Christian life consists essentially in charity. God is love (charity) and to partake of His life is to enter the mainstream of charity. The practice of the moral virtues is simply, first, the regulation of our whole being so as to insure the absolute primacy of charity in our lives, and secondly, it is a striving to meet the exigencies of charity in every department of our lives. Thus all the virtues are "polarized" by charity; they converge on it as a necessary preparation and flow from it as from a source.

Charity is the law of the kingdom of God; it is the very life of God, which grows in us as we practice all the virtues in 'our daily lives. When we enter the kingdom through faith and live according to its law, charity, we are marching with the people of God toward the full realization of the kingdom at the end of time. On that march we are sustained by hope, the eschatological virtue whereby we sense the progress of the kingdom toward the Savior's return.

Seen in this light, the function of hope appears in its original character. Nevertheless, we must try to discern the true nature of hope by studying it according to the methods of classical theology, which is so insistent on clear concepts. For if we disregard the demands of a "theology of essentials," what we gain in "living values" will soon be lost in a lamentable confusion of ideas. However, in making our analysis—which, if you will, may be called "theoretical"— we shall be guided by what we have already learned about the true nature of hope.

2. Hope as a Theological Virtue

In the celebrated phrase of St. Anselm, the role of theology is to use reason enlightened by faith "to reach an understanding of the faith." Hence theology must justify the presence in the supernatural life of the hope revealed by Scripture, and the capital importance which St. Paul gives hope by associating it with faith and charity. "Entities are not to be multiplied without necessity," is a basic rule in theology, as well as in philosophy, and consequently, theology must show the necessity of hope. It does so by establishing the principles of the supernatural life along the lines of the organization of human, natural life.

In the natural order, we are endowed with all the principles necessary to live our lives as men. Our intellect allows us to know *truth*, not only speculative truth, the proper object of intellectual contemplation, but also that practical truth which should guide our conduct in life. Our will, which by nature is completely dynamic, urges us toward the good. But the will is a blind faculty, unable to see or know, for that is not its function. Instead, it loves, desires, wishes, moves. Once it is in the presence of that which is good, it instinctively recognizes it as its proper object. However, this object is presented to the will by the intellect, which alone is capable of seeing. Thus our whole life, which is simply a journey toward happiness and joy, is directed by these two principles, intellect and will. The intellect discovers the good which is the final end of our life and proposes that good to the will, which then reaches out in pursuit of the desired end.

It is at this point that God intervenes to reveal to us a destiny that surpasses all human understanding, to tell us that we are in fact made for a happiness that is beyond the powers of the human will. No longer are we to pursue a merely human destiny but rather the destiny of the sons of God.

From the moment God raises us to the plane of a supernatural destiny that absolutely transcends our natural capacity, the purely human principles which are enough to guide our lives as mere men become insufficient and powerless. Because we are made for God, for a supernatural end, He must give us new supernatural principles. Hence the need for faith, that light which raises our intellect and our knowledge of truth to the supernatural plane, the knowledge of God in Himself and of the whole mystery of our sharing in God's life. Faith, which is a supernatural "intellect," fulfills its role as the eyes of the will, presenting to the will a happiness hitherto unknown, unsuspected, and inaccessible. For faith does not reveal to us a system of theoretical truths or a wisdom that is purely intellectual, but rather the mystery of salvation involving our entire destiny and activity as sons of God.

In this way, the will, which is the faculty of love, desire and conquest, is suddenly brought face to face with the supreme good before which its own powers are helpless. Therefore the will, too, must be elevated and enlarged to the dimensions of infinite happiness. It must be adapted to its new role so that it may be able to love, desire, and possess God Himself by sharing in His very life.

It is the function of the virtues of charity and hope to effect this adaptation. Charity puts the human will in harmony with God, the supreme good, as faith puts the intellect in harmony with infinite truth. But the absolute disproportion between the will and infinite beatitude presents a difficulty. Can we really acquire this infinitely desirable good, the supreme and only aim of our life? Is not such happiness beyond our reach? Is it truly possible for us to acquire it? Or is it not just a wild dream that can never come true? Can we, weak and miserable as we are, really expect this happiness, can we truly *hope* for it? This is where the virtue of hope comes in. For it is hope, based on God's formal promise, on His omnipotence and goodness, that urges us to reach out confidently toward the acquisition of our supreme happiness, the possession of God. This happiness then is attainable because God Himself has promised it to us, because God will give Himself to us as our beatitude.

In seeking to know the role of hope in the supernatural life, we also discover what makes it a virtue, and a theological virtue at that. The proper function of a virtue, which makes good all the acts that proceed from it, is to bring our actions into conformity with the basic rules of human conduct. But God is the supreme rule. Hence, with the exception of faith and charity, hope is more profoundly a virtue than any other because it is truly theological; for not only is it infused into the soul by God alone, as is every supernatural virtue; not only does it direct a part of our activity to God as does every real virtue; it also has God as its direct object. All that it looks forward to, it expects from God as from its only Helper, as the only one through whom it can obtain its goal, which is nothing less than the eternal possession of God Himself.

THE DOUBLE OBJECT OF HOPE

1. The "Motive" of Hope

When speaking of hope, it is usual to distinguish between its *motive* and its *object*. Under *motive* (from *motivum*, "that which moves"), we generally include several distinct elements—God's promise and His faithfulness in fulfilling it, His goodness, or His omnipotence. However, we must note that using the word "motive" can lead to confusion. Hence we prefer to speak, as St. Thomas does, of the double object of hope—the material object, namely, the *thing* attained by hope; and the formal object, that is, the *means* by which hope obtains this thing hoped for, or the support of hope.[1]

We shall reserve the term "motive" for that which moves us to hope, that which makes hope possible in the first place, that which justifies it exteriorly. The motive of hope, then, will be the result of a judgment of hopefulness (*i.e.*, "hope is possible and reasonable"), which leads only to the threshold of theological hope, just as the judgment of credibility justifies the act of faith, as far as that is possible, while still remaining outside faith.

This motive of hope is God's promise, which implies, as a necessary corollary, God's fidelity to His word. It is that alone which allows us to glimpse the possibility of including the possession of God within the scope of our desires. Without this divine promise, supernatural hope is not only impossible but even inconceivable. The bliss of heaven is an absolutely gratuitous gift, and if we were not certain that God offers it to us, we could not legitimately allow ourselves even to desire it.

As can be seen, we have not yet come to hope properly so-called, but are only dealing with the preamble to hope, its exterior motive. Faith provides us with this motive by revealing God's design to us. Hence faith is truly the foundation of hope.

[1] If we compare hope to a lever, then the formal object of hope is the fulcrum.

In order to understand properly the real motive of hope, as justified by an extrinsic reason, we shall examine more closely its *material* and *formal* objects. These terms have the great advantage of enabling us to grasp the unity of the act of hope in its two dynamic aspects because, far from destroying the unity of hope, this double object protects it. There is not one act of hope that terminates in God as the "means" or as the cause-of-our-beatitude, and another act that terminates in God as our beatitude itself. There is only one and the same act which is faced toward God, the only means of our receiving God, infinite beatitude.

These are the two elements that must necessarily make up the movement of hope. Faith presents exactly the same phenomenon. In faith we cleave to God, the First Truth (formal object), in order to attain through Him the material object, namely, revealed truth. Only by submitting our intellect to God, infinite Truth, can we accept the truth of that which is revealed. The two aspects of faith cannot be separated without destroying the virtue itself.

The same holds good for hope: the double object cannot be divided. To attempt to attain divine beatitude without the aid of God, the sole means, is to destroy hope. We also destroy hope if we rely on God, the sole means, in a desire to attain anything else besides divine beatitude. We must now examine this unity of hope in its double object.

2. *The Thing Hoped For* (*Material Object*)

Scripture presents the material object of hope as being extremely rich in content and quite complex. The intellect's insistent demand for unity and clarity has led theologians to analyze the kingdom of God promised to Christians in an endeavor to isolate the exact and essential object of hope. Faith presented the same challenge, which theologians met by selecting, from among all the truths revealed in Scripture, a list of essentials which they designated as articles of faith. In the case of hope, the task was even simpler. All the images which describe the kingdom of God in its perfect state reveal it as perfect happiness for men. St. Paul and St. John speak explicitly about the vision of God face to face, which is obviously the essential element of the kingdom of God, namely, the possession of God in a direct vision and in the closest and most complete union.

A psychological analysis of hope shows that it is at the root of love (love of concupiscence, as we shall see later) and of desire.[2] In other words, hope is a reaching out for an object that is loved and desired, for it is the good as such, i.e., happiness, that arouses love and desire. Hence, it is precisely under the aspect of the good, of happiness, that the object of hope must be conceived. And since it is a question of man's supreme, total, and sole hope in his search for his supernatural destiny, the object of hope must be supreme beatitude. That is why theologians usually do not designate the kingdom of God, but rather its equiva-

---

[2] In his phenomenology of hope, Gabriel Marcel departs on several points from the traditional analysis of this idea. In particular, he is afraid of "a ruinous confusion of hope with desire," which leads to failure to recognize the fact that "hope is bound up with inter-subjectivity," and that hence hope can have only a communal aspect whereby, in his opinion, it diverges from desire and goes far beyond it. See his *Homo Viator* (Chapter entitled "Esquisse d'une phénoménologie et d'une métaphysique de l'espérance"), and *Structure de l'espérance*, in *Dieu vivant*, no. 19, 1951, pp. 73–80.

lent, eternal happiness, as the object of hope. Thus, although the more philosophic idea of supreme happiness is
preferred to the more concrete and complex term used in
Scripture, the reality expressed is exactly the same.

But we must make a distinction. St. Augustine's opinion
that we can hope only for our own good is philosophically
exact. Desire is a movement of appetite which can have as
its object only a personal good, a good proper to the person
desiring. So, too, with hope: I can really hope only for my
own good. Yet this seems to be in contradiction to the
Scriptures because the hope mentioned there is impregnated with "a charity which causes us to break through the
boundaries of our purely individual destinies in order to
unite ourselves with all the other children of God." Hence,
to proceed in an orderly fashion we must distinguish between the object of hope, when hope follows its own movement, and the object of hope, when it is transformed by
charity.

It should be noted, however, that this distinction is valid
particularly on the theoretical plane and makes for greater
precision of ideas because true, complete hope, like any virtue, must be "informed" by charity. Just as faith without
charity is a "dead faith," so also hope without charity (e.g.,
when it exists outside the state of grace), is, if not dead, at
least stunted and devitalized. A good word for it would be
hope "in abeyance."

When we speak of hope left to its own movement, we
do not mean a hope that exists without charity: we simply
wish to stress the contribution that charity makes to the
very heart of the movement of hope.

a.) The Object of Hope Left to Itself

The object of hope by itself is the kingdom of God, eternal life, insofar as it is *my* beatitude. Beatitude is precisely "God possessed"; hence it is both God Himself in His infinite reality (objective aspect) and the act by which I enter into possession of God (subjective aspect). Here again we must preserve perfect unity between the two aspects. Beatitude is essentially God, the Supreme Good, but not considered as a wholly self-subsisting Being since He can be the Supreme Good only in relation to man, the subject of beatitude. Therefore the object of hope can be defined as God, the Supreme Good, insofar as He is my beatitude.

This beatitude is realized essentially in the vision of the divine essence because it is by vision, or perfect knowledge, that we possess God; and this act of possession involves as its immediate corollary the joy of possession. Therefore the body's participation is not absolutely necessary to the essence of beatitude since the spiritual act by which we enjoy the vision of God can be performed without the body. Nevertheless, if beatitude is to be full and complete, it must penetrate the whole man and inundate his entire being. And man is not simply a spirit, but is spirit and matter, soul and body. That is why the resurrection of the body and its participation in the glory of heaven will complete man's beatitude, which will then grow, not in intensity, but in extension by including the body. Moreover, the company of the elect will be a further complement of essential beatitude. As a matter of fact, the friendship of the saints is an element of the happiness of heaven;

it is part of beatitude and hence is part of the material object of hope. All of this is contained in the term "heaven," which is the principal object of hope.

But in its very movement toward beatitude, hope includes in its object, as a secondary element, all that leads to this end. Hope depends on God for the attainment of eternal life and, at the same time, it looks to Him for all the means necessary to reach that goal. Thus everything that leads to the realization of man's supernatural destiny is normally within the field of hope.

Therefore, the object of hope is primarily the whole domain of grace—the increase of habitual grace and the virtues, actual graces, the forgiveness of sins, and the remission of temporal punishment—the indispensable means to, and the necessary condition for, beatitude. Furthermore, the ambit of hope embraces also temporal goods insofar as they are suited to lead us to eternal life. It includes "all these things" which have been promised to us on earth in addition to the bliss of heaven (cf. Matt. 6:33; Luke 12:31). In fact, the object of hope is simply the object of prayer, the things we legitimately pray for, so that prayer has been called "the interpreter of hope."

b.) The Object of Hope Informed by Charity

What we have said so far about the object of hope concerns only *my* personal beatitude. By the unaided movement of hope, I can wish for *my* good alone. Of course, the good of another can be the object of my desire and hope as such, but only insofar as this desire and hope are good for me and contribute to my own happiness.

If I am really to hope for the good of another and not

for myself, I must wish, desire, and hope in his place, as if I were he. I must espouse his cause completely and identify myself with him to the extent of becoming one with him. Now, love effects this union. It implies the union of the lover and the beloved; it is a synthesis of subject and object which is the equivalent, on the affective plane, of the union of subject and object in knowledge.

This union of love can be realized in two ways: (1) The union is effected for the benefit of the subject, the lover. This is the love of concupiscence, the self-interested love, in which the object serves exclusively for the enrichment of the subject, who refers everything to himself. The subject wills his own good. This is the way a person likes wine, traveling, everything that is "useful" or simply "pleasant." (2) The union is effected for the benefit of the object, the beloved, and the subject takes the object as his end, as the value to which he refers himself. This is disinterested love, the love of benevolence or of friendship, wherein the subject wills the good of the object. This is love in its perfect state, or charity.

Self-interested love is at the roots of hope, a point to which we shall return later. For now, we should note that even in its perfect state, love cannot prescind completely from the first aspect, described above, for when I love another for himself and with a disinterested love, my own personal perfection and joy are inseparably bound up with that love.

Hence, necessarily and by its very nature, hope implies love in its "imperfect" form and, of itself, does not have to involve perfect love. Charity will add this element to hope; and, because of the union which charity establishes

between me and the person I love, it will allow me to hope
for that person's happiness insofar as it is *his* happiness as
ardently as if it were my own personal good.

When hope is impregnated with charity, it extends so far
as to desire beatitude for others, and it finds therein the
fullness of its object. In this way we can restore to hope
that amplitude and that "catholic" dimension which it has
in Sacred Scripture.

The Christian was not created to hope all by himself
in his little corner of the world. He is, by nature, a son of
God, bound to God and to all his brethren by divine charity. Although in the interests of scientific analysis we have
distinguished between hope left to itself and hope informed
by charity, we must not try to tear apart the reality of
hope itself. True hope is the hope of the true Christian,
whose very life is charity. Hence the Christian does not
hope solely for his own happiness and his own participation in the kingdom. Rather, he desires, awaits, and hopes
for the perfect realization of the divine plan, that is, for
the coming of God's kingdom in all its glory.

In this way the eschatological element (more specifically,
the *parousia*) finds its rightful place in the object of hope—
of purely "individual" hope and of hope informed by
charity.

Insofar as it involves our resurrection, the coming of the
Lord to inaugurate the perfect kingdom, regarded as the
event in time which the whole Christian people are awaiting, is the object of "individual" hope. In this sense, the
parousia is the necessary complement of the beatitude assured by the vision of God. Since it marks the assembling
of the elect around Christ in His glory, it is part of our

"individual" beatitude, for it assures us of the eternal company of our heavenly friends.

But above all, the *parousia* will complete God's work, and will proclaim the triumph of Christ and His Church, as well as the salvation of the world and of the predestined. It will achieve all the things for which we struggle here below, for which we long with all our strength, and which we desire not for our own benefit but for the glory of God, and out of love for Him and our neighbors. In this sense, the *parousia* is not the object of hope left to its own power, but of hope informed by charity.

Therefore, it is here that the *event*, our Lord's second coming, fits into a complete organization of the object of hope, because the realization of everything that constitutes the proper and necessary object of hope informed by charity is bound up with a precise good—the *parousia*. This event is the concrete, historical object to which hope reaches out.

Through charity, the glory of God and the eternal happiness of our brethren become most dear to our hearts, and because of charity, we include God's glory and our neighbor's happiness within the ambit of our hope. Consequently, we desire and look for the glory of God and the salvation of others with the same eagerness and confidence that we show in our hopes for our own beatitude.

Just as individual hope includes in its object not only the goal of hope but also the means necessary to attain that goal, so also the hope of the Christian who thinks, lives, and acts in full awareness of his incorporation with the Church by charity, embraces not only the final glory of the kingdom of God, but also the development of that kingdom on earth. The Christian has absolute confidence in the unconquerable strength of the Church in her struggles here below. Relying on the divine promise and assured of the energizing presence of the Holy Spirit, he is convinced that the Church will hold her course unflinchingly to the final victory despite the world's assaults, and despite even the weakness of her members. As we have seen, this is the theme of the Apocalypse. Thus in the history of Christianity, hope is the wellspring of true Christian optimism, not of a vague feeling that "everything will turn out all right,"[3] but rather the infallible certitude that the kingdom of God is being established and will remain unconquered despite every persecution.

3. The Basis of Hope (The Formal Object)

In the act of hope which Catholics say, the "motive" of hope is given as God's promise and His fidelity to that promise, or, in the longer form of the act of hope, both the promise and the divine attributes which it involves— "because you are infinitely good, omnipotent, and faithful to your promises."

As a matter of fact, theologians are not agreed as to the true motive for hope. Earlier we made a distinction between the motive and the formal object of hope. It now remains for us to find out what is the precise formal object of hope, what exactly is the "means" upon which hope relies to attain its end. We know that this object, this

[3] See the opposition which Gabriel Marcel sets up between hope and optimism in *Homo Viator* in the chapter entitled, "Esquisse d'une phénoménologie, et d'une métaphysique du l'espérance."

"means," is God, but we wish to ascertain exactly which of God's attributes is the basis of hope.

Some theologians believe that it is God's goodness (thus Duns Scotus and Suárez, who stress the aspect of desire found in hope). For others (St. Thomas, St. Bonaventure, Vásquez and the majority of Thomistic theologians), it is "the divine assistance," or, more precisely, God's assisting omnipotence. Still others believe that it is God, insofar as He is our good, and His assisting omnipotence. This last opinion is obviously a synthesis of the two preceding ones; apparently it had the support of Cajetan and Bañez (see Ripalda and the Jesuit theologians in general). Finally, some theologians, anxious to omit nothing, mention God's omnipotence, goodness, and fidelity (St. Alphonsus, Tanquerey).[4]

Moreover, all these theories are further subdivided, and it would not be possible to discuss them here one by one. We know that, on the whole, God's promise plays the role of exterior and preliminary motive. But if we are to grasp the internal motive, or better, the formal object of hope, we must recall the nature of the movement of the virtue. This movement is not simply a desire; if that were so, then the aspect of goodness would hold primacy of place in the object of hope. Instead, hope goes beyond desire to await confidently an object, the possession of which is surrounded with a certain atmosphere of uncertainty. Hence all the strength of hope must be concentrated on overcoming this initial uncertainty. All its potential of confidence rests in this "emotional conviction" that it will attain its object be-

[4] In an article entitled "Espérance" in *Dictionnaire de Théologie Catholique*, S. Harent describes and evaluates the different systems.

cause it relies absolutely on Him who alone can allow it to reach that object.

Thus we hope for God because we hope *in* Him and because we leave in His hands the whole reason for our confidence. He alone is powerful enough to lead us to our end, the possession of that which we hope for. It seems, therefore, that the mainspring of the movement of hope, the element that gives it its perfect confidence and guarantees its efficacy, is the omnipotence of God, which is placed at our service. That is what is meant by the divine assistance or, as we saw, more exactly, God's assisting omnipotence. But be that as it may, one thing is certain: God alone is capable of giving us possession of God. He alone is the refuge of hope.

Acting in the fullness of His infinite perfection, which is diffused in all creation, God enables His creatures to be, in their turn, the cause of other beings. In like manner, He grants to certain beings the dignity of becoming bases for hope. It is true that these created beings are depositories of hope only secondarily and, as God's instruments, receiving all their efficacy from Him. Yet we can truly hope *in* them also.

First among them is the human nature which the Second Person of the Blessed Trinity assumed in the work of our redemption. Then there is the whole life of the Church— grace, the sacraments, the gifts of God. Men, too, have been called to cooperate effectively in the salvation of their brethren and in preparing for the coming of the glorious kingdom—the saints in heaven with the Blessed Virgin as their Queen and those people on earth whom God has placed along our way to be His helpers. All these are, by

God's will, truly the sustainers of our hope and we have every right to place our trust in them, too.

It is in this perspective that we can see how our own merits fit into the formal object or cause of our hope. Granted that we must not glory in our merits or forget that they, too, are God's gratuitous gifts, yet we must recognize in them the mercy of God leading us to eternal glory and we should see that by gaining merit we are truly cooperating with Him in the work of our final destiny.

4. The Real Meaning of Christian Hope

Now that we have determined the object of hope and the basis upon which it rests (the formal object), we can assemble the elements of genuine Christian hope, completely impregnated with divine charity.

Hope is, in a sense, the link between faith and charity. It is closely related to faith and, like faith, it is centered on an object which is still absent. Faith does not see, but has a provisional or waiting function, since it is a preparation for the beatific vision, before which it will fade. So, too, does hope await the possession of its desired object, a possession which is still deferred; it looks forward to the full possession of God, at the threshold of which it will disappear. Hope also resembles charity in that it is not essentially knowledge, as is faith, but rather a movement of the will, full of love, desire, and joy. That is why it naturally leads the soul toward charity or pure love, as we shall see later.

Nevertheless, to be genuine and perfect, hope must presuppose both faith and charity. Therein lies the mystery of the complex relationship between the virtues, or rather, the mystery of the wonderful unity of the three theological virtues, which we approach in a variety of ways but do not fully attain. Faith provides hope with its object because it is faith that first brings us into the presence of God, for whom we hope. Once based on this knowledge of the God of love and of joy, hope can reach out for Him under its own power. In the same way, hope presupposes charity. It is independent of charity and, at least basically, it can fulfill itself without charity. But, as we have seen, if it is to reach its full dimensions and realize all its potentialities, it must allow itself to be impregnated with charity.

Thus the Christian is enlightened by faith and placed in the presence of God, who is proposed to him as the supreme good and who is infinitely capable of fulfilling all his desires. He already loves God, because true faith implies love, and now he begins to desire Him, not ineffectually and as an impossible dream, but, with all the strength of his soul, which was made to see God, he reaches out towards Him, the supreme good. This is no longer hope because it goes beyond desire, although it presupposes it. God Himself has given His word. He has promised man this eternal, blissful union with Him in the glorious kingdom. The man who believes in God and loves Him as his supreme good has only to trust himself absolutely to God and to rely wholly on Him in order to live his whole life without fear, with an unshakable confidence, and in the certainty of victory, He trusts God to give him everything and to help him overcome every obstacle. He knows that God is not only the fulfillment of all his desires for happiness, but that He is also infinitely worthy of complete, disinterested love for His own sake. In this way, the Christian enters fully into charity and at the same time his hope expands to its fullest measure. By charity his will becomes one with God's will so that he loves and wills what God wills. But he is still a pilgrim on earth and God's work is not yet finished. The completion of this work is the object of his hope.

Therefore, he relies on the divine promise; through charity he regards everything from God's point of view, making his will one with God's; he loves and wills the good of his brethren as much as his own; he trusts in God with all his heart and confidently expects the accomplishment of all God's works at the end of his earthly battle, in which God's grace sustains him. He hastens joyfully towards the crowning of God's work in his own life, and his hope finds expression in the words of St. Paul, "I desire to depart and to be with Christ" (*cf.* Phil. 1:23). But he also goes forward in the joy of charity and in unity of heart with all the sons of God toward the glorious day of Christ's final victory, toward God's absolute dominion over a renewed world. In other words, he marches with head erect and radiant countenance toward the day of the Lord's return, and his hopeful prayer is that of the Apocalypse: "Come, Lord Jesus!"

HOPE AND CHARITY

Faith, hope, and charity form the trilogy of the theological virtues. Faith supplies hope with its object, and without faith, hope is not possible. But the relationship between hope and charity is less simple since these two virtues are closer to each other and resemble each other more than they resemble faith, because they are both virtues of the will and each is a love of God.

1. The Love of Hope and the Love of Charity

We have already discussed the difference between these two concepts: the love that is the basis for hope is a "self-interested" love, a love of concupiscence, whereas the love of charity is disinterested, a love of benevolence. In the love of hope, I will my own good, my personal happiness, and I will and desire everything else insofar as it is connected with my happiness. In the love of charity, I love God for Himself; I do not refer Him to something else but rest in my love for Him.

We must point out that love does not occupy as important a place in hope as it does in charity. There is a love at the basis of my hope, the love of a good which I do not possess and which therefore arouses the desire of possession, the love of a good the acquisition of which presents difficulties that I can surmount only by relying on God's power, from which I draw my unwavering confidence. All these elements are essential to hope. But on the contrary, love is not merely one of the elements of charity, for charity is *essentially* love. In itself, charity prescinds from the possession or nonpossession of its object. The charity which we have toward God in this life will not change its nature when we see Him face to face. But hope will disappear because it will no longer have any reason for existence.

For the rest, the difference between these two loves will suffice to distinguish clearly between hope and charity. The love of hope, then, is a "self-interested" love which seeks its own happiness and which, therefore, is imperfect. But again we must understand these terms correctly.

The love of hope is supernatural, as is that of charity.

Man cannot love God as his beatitude or as the good which fills all his expectations of happiness unless God is revealed to him and unless he is made capable by a supernatural virtue of loving and desiring Him. Hence, while we say that the love of hope is imperfect, we must remember at the same time, that it is perfectly supernatural.

Compared to the love of charity, which is the perfect and finished form of love, the love of hope is indeed *imperfect*. But that does not by any means signify that it is not a true love or that it is a love which necessarily contains an inherent defect. The love of hope is legitimate and, what is more, it is essential.

Many people, desirous of correcting and purifying hope in this respect, have only succeeded in destroying it. The Church has reacted vigorously against such errors by affirming the lawfulness of this "self-interested" love. Condemning Luther's teaching, the Council of Trent proclaimed: "If anyone shall say that the justified man sins when he does good works with a view to an eternal reward; let him be anathema." [5]

Jansen and his disciples, especially Quesnel, held that the movement of hope toward beatitude was legitimate only if it was supported by the disinterested love of charity. According to them, it is not lawful to love and desire God insofar as He is our beatitude: "Whoever serves God with a view to an eternal reward, if he lacks charity, is not free from fault as often as he acts with a view to eternal happiness." [6]

At the end of the seventeenth century, Molinos, the

[5] See Denziger, *Enchiridion Symbolorum*, no. 841.
[6] Proposition condemned by Alexander VIII; Denziger, *op. cit.*, no. 1303.

father of Quietism, taught that it is unworthy of perfect souls to retain the smallest particle of self-interested love in their hope. Pope Innocent XI explicitly condemned this proposition of Molinos: "He who has given his free will to God should care about nothing, neither about hell nor heaven; nor ought he to desire his own perfection or virtues or his own sanctity or his own salvation, the hope of which he ought to expunge." [7]

Fénelon, espousing the cause of "pure love," wished that, in those who are perfect, hope should be as disinterested as charity itself. Many propositions taken from his *Explications des maximes des saints sur la vie intérieure*, which was published in Paris in 1697, were condemned by Pope Innocent XII in 1699. For example:

> There is an habitual state of the love of God which is pure charity without any admixture of a motive of personal interest. Neither fear of punishment nor desire of reward has a place in it any longer. God is no longer loved in view of merit or one's own perfection, or because of the happiness that is to be found in loving him. [8]

And he later speaks of "perfect hope, that is, the disinterested desire for the promises." [9]

In condemning these theories, the Church was simply protecting the nature of the virtue of hope. She also affirmed the legitimacy of "self-interested" love, which must not, however, be understood to mean that we may use God solely as a means to satisfy our thirst for happiness.

[7] *Idem*, no. 1232.
[8] *Idem*, no. 1327.
[9] *Idem*, no. 1337.

That would be to debase God and use Him for an end inferior to Him, namely, man. Such an intention would make our love for God unlawful. But to love God as our beatitude is, on the contrary, to make Him the ultimate end of our lives, to direct all our activity to Him and to choose Him as our final destiny. It means turning with our whole heart to God as our supreme and only good.

As St. Francis de Sales points out in his *Treatise on the Love of God:*

> We do not draw God to us for our own benefit, but rather join ourselves to Him as to our final happiness. . . . When we love God as our sovereign good, we do not bring Him to us but ourselves to Him; we are not His end . . . , rather He is ours. He does not belong to us; we belong to Him. He does not depend on us; we depend on Him.

Therefore, such a love is not only lawful; it is necessary. Our main duty, which is inscribed in our very nature as rational, free beings, is to tend in all our actions to our ultimate end, beatitude. This desire for our ultimate end holds sway over our whole moral life. We must make God, and God alone, our happiness. But the love of hope is simply the love of God as our beatitude, as the ultimate end of our life. This self-interested love is so necessary that even the perfection of love, the love of charity, by which we will love God and give ourselves unreservedly to Him, will not destroy the aspect of self-interest in our love, for it will always be true that the God whom we love for His infinite perfection will be our beatitude, the ultimate end of our life, the only One who can fulfill the gnawing desire for happiness which is part of our nature.

2. Hope Informed by Charity

Nevertheless, the love which regards God as the infinite good cannot be satisfied with a motive of self-interest. When faced with Supreme Beauty, Perfection and Goodness, love must expand into a great happiness, a joyful contemplation and a full gift of self in which there is not the least trace of self-seeking. Thus hope leads to charity. There is in the love of hope a call to a nobler love, to that unconditional love of God in which alone love can reach the fullness of its nature.

Hope can exist without charity, but, like faith, it is then a "dead virtue." If hope remains alone, without leading to charity, it limits the development of love, for love tends with all its strength toward meeting its own noblest requirements.

In its turn, charity reacts on hope to give it a new perfection. But it does not substitute its own love for that of hope, which would mean destroying the love of hope. Charity respects the nature of hope and does not take away hope's object or divert its action. Rather charity develops the love of hope side by side with the other love, the supreme and perfect love of charity.

Hence hope and charity concur in developing the double aspect of love and, what is more, charity expands the object of hope to its ultimate dimensions, causing us to look beyond the narrow horizon of our personal salvation, lifting us above the search for our own happiness. In a sense, charity identifies us with God and our neighbor by a unity of affection to the point where the divine good as such and the good of the neighbor as such are introduced into the object of hope.

When we love God and our neighbor with a full and disinterested love of charity, we are borne toward their good by the same movement that launches us on the search for our own happiness. Of course, strictly speaking we cannot hope for God's happiness since it is not a future object nor is it impeded by any obstacle, but we can hope for the perfect manifestation of God's glory in the final triumph of Christ and His Church. We can truly hope for our neighbor's happiness and for his eternal salvation after the vicissitudes of this life. Therefore by impregnating hope, charity raises it to its full stature. Far from destroying or supplanting it, charity gives hope a new expansion, perfecting and crowning it.

7

The Virtue of the Pilgrim of God

✠

RISK AND ASSURANCE

"So there abide faith, hope and charity, these three; but the greatest of these is charity" (1 Cor. 13:13). Faith and hope are the virtues to be practiced by those who are making their way toward God, whom they do not yet see or possess; but charity is eternal.

By its very nature, hope is a virtue which belongs exclusively to men on earth. The damned do not hope because eternal punishment necessarily includes the certainty that nothing can ever alleviate its implacable severity. Dante was a good theologian when he wrote over the threshold of his *Inferno:* "Abandon hope, all ye who enter here." Hatred and absolute despair are the lot of the damned.

Nor do the blessed in heaven practice true theological hope, for they now possess that which they hoped for during their earthly lives. They now see God and have the perfect joy of being united to him without any fear of ever losing Him. True, they still desire and await the resurrection of the body, which will complete their beatitude. Yet because they possess God they have the absolute certainty that everything else will come to them in due time as an infallible consequence.[1] They are no longer subject to the condition of those who live in fervent confidence, but who are exposed by their weakness to the danger of falling.

That is the reason why hope is characteristic of man on earth. Hope is made up of certainty and uncertainty, of solid conviction and steadfastness, but also of a disquiet that will remain until death. We've already quoted the proverb, "While there's life, there's hope." We can also say, "While there's life, there's *only* hope." While we are on earth, we can have only a hope of happiness and not absolute certainty. That is our lot as men.

Insofar as our hope relies on God, it is infallible because there is no danger that God will fail us. Therein lies the certainty of hope. However, "certainty" must not be understood here in the intellectual sense. Properly speaking, certainty, or certitude, belongs to the realm of knowledge and it can be applied to the affective sphere analogically only. The certainty in hope is, more exactly, an "affective conviction," a "will to certitude," based entirely on God's omnipotence and unfailing fidelity.

[1] There is some controversy among theologians about the existence of hope in Christ and the saints. There is an interesting study by P. Charles entitled, "Spes Christi," in *Nouvelle Revue Théologique*, 1934 and 1937.

However, there still remains in hope a margin of uncertainty, a danger of nonfulfillment, which is an essential element and a necessary aspect of hope. When we are completely certain that we shall obtain something, we do not hope for it but simply wait for it: we have the serene assurance that we shall possess it. Here there is none of that hardening of resolve, that bracing of oneself so characteristic in the difficult struggle to acquire an object that may elude one's grasp. When Luther taught that men can be saved only through the absolute certainty of their salvation, an unconditional certainty that came entirely from the superabundant justice of Christ, he not only denied the least autonomy of free will but also completely distorted the nature of hope. For hope can have only a fervent "certainty" which always contains some disquiet. As long as hope has not attained full possession of its object, the soul cannot enjoy perfect repose; and possession of the object causes hope to cease. As St. Augustine has truly said, "Our hearts are restless until they rest in Thee."

Our restlessness and uncertainty do not come from God, but from ourselves, from our weakness and inconstancy. We have not the absolute certainty that we shall persevere to the end, as the Council of Trent explicitly reminds us.

It must not be said that those who are truly justified should be convinced without any doubt whatsoever, that they are justified . . . as if anyone who does not so believe doubts God's promises and the efficacy of Christ's death and resurrection. For, just as no pious person should doubt God's mercy, the merit of Christ and the power and efficacy of the sacraments, so every person when he considers himself and his own weakness and lack of proper dispositions, can be apprehensive about, and fear for, his own grace since no one can know, with the certainty of faith, which cannot be subject to error, that he has received the grace of God.[2]

In particular, the gift of final perseverance cannot be the subject of absolute certainty:

> Similarly in regard to the gift of perseverance, of which it is written: "He who has persevered to the end will be saved" (Matt. 10:22, 24:13), let no one promise himself anything as certain with absolute certainty, although all should place and repose the firmest hope in God's help.[3]

Again on this point, the Council of Trent expressly defined that: "If anyone shall say that he will certainly have, with an absolute and infallible certainty, that great gift of perseverance to the end, unless he shall have learned it from a special revelation: let him be anathema."[4]

This is so because we are endowed with freedom and, despite the efficacy of divine grace, are essentially weak and always liable to fall. That is the tragedy of our human nature, and from it spring all the disquiet and uncertainty in hope. As long as we are not established in eternal life by the vision of God, we are capable of sinning. The certainty of our hope comes from God; the uncertainty from ourselves. Such is our condition while we are on earth: we tend toward God fervently and steadfastly, with the greatest infallibility insofar as God alone is concerned, but with the most abysmal weakness insofar as our human frailty is involved.

[2] Denziger, *op. cit.*, no. 802.
[3] *Idem.*, no. 806.
[4] *Idem.*, no. 826.

This contrast enables us to see the true nature and basic character of hope since it shows the indispensable role which the virtue plays in our pursuit of our destiny. Those who trust only in themselves, who look for the meaning of human destiny only in the unassisted exercise of free will, which fails so easily, and who wish to follow only "the path of freedom" and refuse outright all help from above—these can end only in despair. They are tortured by their thirst for happiness, but when they find that they cannot quench this thirst by their own unaided powers, they despair; and their despair is all the greater the more sincerely and consciously they have striven to reach their goal. Then they taste the bitterness that lies behind the words of Albert Camus in *Caligula*: "Men die and are not happy."

The whole of contemporary atheistic existentialism echoes with the heart-rending cry of infinite despair. Yet we need to catch a glimpse of a world without hope if we are to understand the preponderant role which hope plays in the Christian concept of destiny. Like the atheists, we, too, know that when man is left to his own resources, he is much more likely to become a brute than a hero; in our cowardice and betrayals, in our repeated resolutions and brave new beginnings which come to nothing, we, too, have assessed the fundamental misery of mankind.

But despite all that, we know that we have hope and that our hope is not vain or deceptive. We are certain that it will lead us to our goal and that we are made for a supernatural destiny full of wonder—the possession of God Himself. We place our trust in God alone, in God who will not fail us and who cannot deceive. That is why hope supports all our efforts, sustains us in our struggles, gives us the courage to bear our burdens, and strengthens our will in a fervent ascent which will lead infallibly to eternal happiness if we do not place any obstacle to God's grace.

HOPE IN DAILY LIFE

As we said at the beginning of this book, we are buoyed up by hopes of all sorts in our everyday life and we cannot do without them. We need hope as much as we need food. Therefore, the Christian must live each day by hope, every moment drawing on this reservoir of energy even for the most commonplace actions. Let us consider some of the occasions when hope is most needed.

We need hope when we recognize the fact that we are sinners. If we are to be saved, we must first acknowledge our need for redemption. But when we first become aware of our state as sinners, we feel humiliated and are tempted to be discouraged because we have no taste for living without self-esteem and without some illusions about ourselves.

Complete sincerity and its inseparable companion, true humility, are difficult virtues to practice because it is hard for us to see ourselves as we really are. And when a sincere self-appraisal uncovers in our lives our amazing mixture of good will, moral misery, calculated self-seeking, ulterior motives and deep-seated corruption, we are tempted to despair. Absolute sincerity with ourselves can scarcely lead to anything but despair—or the most complete hope.

This is so because we know that we are sinners and that, if bitter experience is any guide, we will very likely remain so to the end. But we also know that God has come to free us from sin and that Christ died to deliver us from evil. We know that God loves us and calls us, sinners though we are. That is where we experience real hope, in the very knowledge that we are sinners. If we thought we were holy and virtuous, we would rely on our holiness and virtue and could not trust in God alone. We must be poor in the Gospel sense if we are to enter fully into the movement of hope. Perhaps the most absolute hope arises out of the deepest distress, when there is no refuge left except God's infinite goodness and His merciful omnipotence: "Out of the depths I cry to thee, O Lord . . . ! In the Lord do I hope, my soul hopes in his word" (Ps. 129).

We need hope when we see our weakness in the face of a difficult task. Even if we want to put sin aside and live as true sons of God, weakness or cowardice weighs us down like heavy shackles. We see what we ought to do, but, without really knowing why, we don't do it, as if there were in us a permanent separation between knowledge and action, as if we were in a state of split consciousness. Even St. Paul himself admitted wearily, as it were: "I do not do the good that I wish, but the evil that I do not wish, that I perform" (Rom. 7:19). And it does not suffice for us to make a firm resolution once and for all: we must begin again and again. That is human nature, of course; but it is very wearisome!

Here again we need the experience of our human weakness so that we may understand what hope is, namely, the total reliance of our misery on God's unfailing strength. If we are to throw ourselves completely on God's mercy, we need to have touched the bottom of human frailty and we must recall from time to time that God has been able to make saints of people who, at the beginning, were no better than we are now. In this way, what seems to be an obstacle to hope can, in fact, become the best occasion for it.

Even suffering can be an occasion for hope. For instance, the invalid stretched on a bed of pain as on a cross, without human hope and apparently useless, can still hope because he knows that he can contribute more than many healthy active persons to "hastening" the establishment of the kingdom of God. Similarly those who are separated from their loved ones by circumstances or even by death, have the assurance that their love will be resumed eternally in heaven with God: "the sufferings of the present time are not worthy to be compared with the glory to come that will be revealed in us" (Rom. 8:18).

There is another kind of suffering which is, for some people, keener than bodily pain or separation, and that is the pain of seeing others suffer. The helplessness we feel when we consider how much poverty, injustice, and criminal stupidity there is in the world can easily beget in us a spirit of revolt or cause us to throw up our hands in despair. For it is a fact that we often accept our own sufferings more patiently than we do those of others, particularly when those others are the victims of injustice.

Only hope, founded on faith, can give us the strength to bear the weight of the tragic conditions in the world; only hope can give us the assurance that the mystery of suffering will be solved, that it will all lead somewhere, that all the problems will find adequate solutions in "a new earth . . . wherein dwells justice,"[5] and that one day

[5] 2 Pet. 3:13; see below, Advent, the Liturgical Season of Hope.

men's tears will be wiped away in the eternal joy of God. Truly, hope is the mainstay of the Christian life on earth.

THE FEAR OF GOD

1. Fear and Hope

Since the Middle Ages, when theological *Summae* were so popular, it has been customary to link the seven gifts of the Holy Ghost with the various virtues. However, the connections made between the gifts and the virtues have not always been very rigorous, and seem to have been inspired mainly by a desire for symmetrical arrangement. Still, the theological virtues have been treated properly in this respect, and the grouping of the gifts with the individual theological virtues seems to have been done on the basis of real relationships. Thus the gifts of understanding and knowledge are grouped with faith, wisdom with charity, and hope with the fear of the Lord.[6] There is no doubt that the gift of fear and the virtue of hope are very closely linked together and that they are complementary movements.

Even on the natural, emotional plane, hope and fear are in some ways parallel, for they both arise from the same source, the "irascible appetite," whence they move sym-

[6] Even in the writings of St. Thomas there is an evolution of doctrine on the relationship between the gifts and the theological virtues, especially the connection between the gift of fear of the Lord and hope. In his first writings he does not connect any of the gifts with the theological virtues, but does link the gift of fear with the moral virtue of temperance (*Sententiae*); later, he makes a reference to hope in relation to the gift of fear (*Summa Theologica*, Ia Pars); and finally he attributes the gift principally to hope (*Idem*, IIa Pars).

metrically toward opposite objects. Hope goes out to a good which it confidently expects to attain; yet there is in it a certain disquiet, a "fear" that it will not reach its goal. Fear is centered on an evil which it dreads but which it nevertheless "hopes" to escape. Thus the two acts are complementary; we are always a little afraid that we shall not get the things we hope for, and we are always hopeful of avoiding the things we fear.

This correlation between hope and fear on the emotional plane is paralleled on the theological plane by the connection between the virtue of hope and the gift of fear of the Lord.

It will be helpful here if we recall the basic role which hope plays throughout the Old Testament. Hope was the underlying theme in the development of Israel. The whole history of the Jews was centered on a hope: they were marching toward God and they looked to Him for everything. Yet, if there is any one idea that stands out in the spirituality of the Old Testament, that idea is the fear of God, which expresses and sums up all man's dealings with God and places them in their proper perspective. This fear of God covers a wide range of feelings from the most instinctive reverential terror to disinterested love. The juxtaposition of hope and fear in the Old Testament is very significant. When we examine the foundations of the fear of the Lord, we find that the main element in it is the sense of God's absolute transcendence, a transcendence which is manifested principally in His omnipotence. We have already seen that the formal motive for hope is the divine omnipotence, insofar as God places it at our disposal. Therefore, the divine attribute, omnipotence, which arouses in us the fear of God is also the attribute that justifies and sustains our hope in Him. The connection between fear and hope will appear even closer when we examine the gift of fear in more detail.

2. The Gift of Fear

If it is true that the object of fear is some evil, how then can we speak about the fear of God, especially in connection with a spiritual gift? How can God, who is the Supreme Good in whom there is no evil, become the object of fear? It is correct to say that an evil is the object of fear, and hence God cannot be truly feared. But fear normally goes beyond the evil that is its direct object and includes the person from whom the evil can come. And God can be a source of evil or at least the occasion of an evil for us, either the evil of the punishment which we deserve for our sins and which God in His justice inflicts on us, or the evil of sin itself which separates us from God, and which is the greatest misfortune that could befall us.

We are considering here only the fear that can bring us closer to God and turn us toward Him; for there is another, ignoble, kind of fear which makes us want to hide from God. But although these two types of fear are good and virtuous, the very diverse motives which inspire them give them very dissimilar characteristics.

When we regard God only as the avenger of sin, as the one who has the power to punish us, our fear of Him is *servile*, the fear which the servant or the slave feels as he stands trembling before his incorruptible master. It is the sinner's fear of infallible justice; it is a salutary fear because it inspires a horror of sin; yet there is little nobility in it.

On the other hand, the fear of sin because it separates us from God, our supreme good, springs from love and is an expression of love. This is *filial* fear, the fear of a son who does not want to displease his father and who is more afraid of losing his father's love than of anything else. St. Augustine calls this "chaste fear," the fear of the bride that she will be parted from her beloved, that she will no longer be able to merit his esteem and tenderness. For the bride, this would be the greatest of evils because her whole happiness consists in her union with her beloved.

Obviously, servile fear is not imbued with the spirit of hope. If we feel toward God only the terror of a slave who is threatened with punishment, we are not likely to turn confidently to Him as to a loving Father who is ready to grant us all our desires. This fear is not a gift of the Holy Spirit; only filial fear constitutes the gift.

The gifts are those special perfections which the Holy Spirit infuses into the soul and which make it fully docile to the divine inspirations and completely malleable under the hands of God. The natural man's guide to action is his reason, which is the reflection of the divine mind, while the Christian's guide is also his reason, but reason enlightened by faith and divinized by grace, for God Himself intervenes directly in the life of His children in order to inspire, guide, and urge them on. The Holy Spirit is truly the Christian's inner guide and teacher in the spiritual life. He directs the attentive soul by His impulses and by His supra-rational inspirations. But the soul must be made sensitive to these inspirations; it must be attuned to God's voice and it must keep its eyes fixed unwaveringly on Him.

This docility is effected by the gifts, and it is specifically the gift of fear that completes and intensifies the theological movement of hope because filial fear cannot but launch the soul wholeheartedly toward Him whom it is afraid of losing. In a sense, the gift of fear is the negative form of hope.

Actually, the gift of fear contains two movements, and it is by means of these movements that hope leads to the mystical life.

First there is the fear of being separated from God. The whole life of the Christian tends toward final union with God, his supreme good. To lose God forever is the irreparable failure, the ruin of our vocation to love and joy; it is eternal woe. Essentially, hell consists in the loss of God. And we lose God only through sin. Hence the gift of fear, which is imbued with the full force of the love of charity, causes us to hate and flee from sin as the greatest of evils. Yet at the same time, this gift leads us to cast ourselves trustingly into God's arms because when we are faced with temptation and the mysterious fascination of evil, we become acutely aware of our weakness and we realize that we are always liable to fall or stray from the straight and narrow path. We feel that we are essentially unstable and that we have no certain claim to holiness or sure hope of salvation—all of which must come to us from God. He alone is infinitely powerful, He alone is holy, He alone can guard us from evil and from ourselves. When we see that, then our fear of being separated from God causes us to turn unconditionally to Him for help. There is no longer any room for presumption on our part: with infinite abandonment and confidence, we look to God for everything.

The second element in fear makes us dread not only being separated from God but also makes us apprehensive of regarding ourselves as equal to God, of comparing ourselves with Him, and of considering that we are of some value in His presence. In short, the gift of fear makes us conscious of our state as creatures. That is why fear can truly be called reverential since it is the source of that inner reverence which nourishes the virtue of religion. Even apart from the possibility that we may sin, we fear God and reverence Him by fleeing with horror from the idea of daring to compare ourselves with Him, of weighing our own worth against Him. The fear of separation will disappear in heaven because then we shall be united with God forever and shall be incapable of sin. But we shall always fear Him with reverential fear as the angels do, for reverential fear is essentially the basic attitude of a creature before its Creator. It is the creature's awareness of his nothingness and of the inaccessible majesty of God, an awareness which he expresses by the deepest reverence.

This profound and reasoned awareness of our littleness before God's sovereign omnipotence, which is undoubtedly the supreme act of the gift of fear, causes our hope to expand to its farthest limits. For we must see the infinite abyss between the Creator and the creature, between the All-Holy God and the sinner by nature, if we are to understand the prodigious character of the hope to which God calls us. Only when our holy fear shows us what God is and what we ourselves are, only then are we able to understand that our confidence in God can never be absolute and deep enough. We must plumb the depths of this reverence if we are to extend our hope to its limit, or rather, if we are to understand that hope has no limits. Only the gift of fear can bring theological hope to the perfection which it displays in the mystical life, mainly in the "ways" which great saints have followed, namely, abandonment to God and spiritual childhood.

ADVENT, THE LITURGICAL SEASON OF HOPE

In a sense, our whole Christian life is a liturgy, which the Church wishes us to adapt to the rhythm of her own cycle of liturgical seasons. In the liturgical year, in which we relive the religious history of mankind in a gripping summary, Advent is the season most characterized by hope. So true is this that, although the word "Advent" means "coming, arrival," we see in it especially the idea of joyous expectation, with all that this implies of desire and impatient hope.

But what are we expecting? What are we waiting for in Advent? The most obvious answer is that we are waiting for the Christmas season, that we are preparing for the feast of the Nativity. But exactly which Christmas season and which Nativity are we waiting for? The birth of Christ two thousand years ago, or the liturgical feast of December 25?

The liturgy of Advent recalls the great tidings of the prophets and the centuries-long expectation of the Jewish people, and it invites us to relive the hope that was the support of Israel. Sustained and guided by the Messianic texts of the Old Testament, we, too, await the coming of the Messias and we sigh for deliverance. Yet while we do this, at the back of our minds there is a certain uneasiness. No doubt Advent means all we have said it does. This is its primary significance and no one who has ever opened a Missal or Breviary would dream of denying it. But the Savior for whom Advent makes us wait was born twenty centuries ago; the Messias has already appeared; He has redeemed His people and has even ascended once more into heaven. Then why are we waiting? We are no longer in Old Testament times, and the life of the Church cannot be reversed any more than history can. The Jews' expectation has been fulfilled and is therefore ended. And if our Christian instinct is correct in regarding Advent as a period of expectancy, that expectancy cannot be merely symbolical.

It is certainly good, and even necessary, to relive the hope of Israel as the liturgy urges us to: "Drop down dew, ye heavens, from above, and let the clouds rain the just; let the earth be opened, and bud forth a savior" (Isa. 45:8). Our whole destiny as children of God, the whole history of mankind is linked to this central event. But, as we have said, this event has occurred. How, then, without falsifying the meaning of Christian history, can we ask modern men to wait anxiously and impatiently for the birth of Christ? We can ask them to assume the point of view of the ancient Jews, who were their forerunners in faith and hope; but then they will sigh for the coming of the Messias only in image, symbol, and memory. Yet the liturgy and the life of the Church which it expresses are more than a mere memorial. The life of the Church is a dynamic reality.

Since Christ came to bring us divine life, this life must increase in us and, through us, in the world at large, as the liturgy of Advent unceasingly reminds us.[7] Just as the Jews looked for the Messias, so also must we continually prepare ourselves for, and be receptive to, His "coming in grace." He must come in us by a deeper penetration of His life into our lives so that we can say with St. Paul: "It is now no longer I that live, but Christ lives in me" (Gal. 2:20). By this "mystical" and wholly interior coming, our Saviour and Lord fills ever more with His presence and makes fruitful by His action His Body, which is the Church; He nourishes from within the life of the kingdom on earth; and His dominion over the world is deepened.

This is no arbitrary interpretation, for all of this comes well within the ambit of hope. These are the fruits of the coming of the Messias, for the Incarnation did not simply stop short; rather it is still being prolonged and extended gradually to its fullest extent. Everything will finally have to be "re-established in Christ" (cf. Eph. 1:10), and hope is fulfilled by the progress of the Church through the ages and by the uninterrupted succession of generations of Christians. Gradually, the true face of the world is being fashioned and it will one day be revealed; and man grows toward his "perfect stature" (cf. Eph. 4:13).

Nevertheless, from the first Sunday in Advent on, the Gospel texts announce another coming, one that we are now thoroughly familiar with: "And then they will see the Son of Man coming upon a cloud with great power and majesty. But when these things begin to come to pass, look up, and lift up your heads, because your redemption is at hand" (Luke 21:27–28). This is the fulfillment of the Christian Advent, the return of Christ. Thus the Advent

[7] See P. Parsch, *The Liturgical Year*, Vol. I, *The Christmas Cycle.*

liturgy shares the same perspective as true hope, for it, too, looks toward our Lord's second coming.

Of course, it is hard for us to feel the same impatience as the first generations of Christians, who were so struck by certain mysterious words of our Lord that they lived in almost feverish expectation of His return. For example, St. Paul had to warn the Thessalonians against jumping to unwarranted conclusions:

> We beseech you, brethren, by the coming of our Lord Jesus Christ and our being gathered together unto Him, not to be hastily shaken from your right mind, nor terrified, whether by spirit, or by utterance, or by letter attributed to us, as though the day of the Lord were near at hand. Let no one deceive you in any way, for the day of the Lord will not come unless the apostasy comes first, and the man of sin is revealed . . . (2 Thess. 2:1–3).

For his part, St. Peter forestalled the criticism and mockery of those who emphasize God's delay in bringing about His Son's return. In a sense, St. Peter excuses our Lord for making us wait for Him:

> This first you must know, that in the last days there will come deceitful scoffers, men walking according to their own lusts, saying, "Where is the promise of his coming? For since the fathers fell asleep, all things continue as they were from the beginning of creation." . . . But, beloved, do not be ignorant of this one thing, that one day with the Lord is as a thousand years, and a thousand years as one day. The Lord does not delay in his promises, but for your sake is longsuffering, not wishing that any should perish but that all should turn to repentance. But the day of the Lord will come as a thief; at that time the heavens will pass away with great

violence, and the elements will be dissolved with heat, and the earth, and the works that are in it, will be burned up. Seeing therefore that all these things are to be dissolved, what manner of men ought you to be in holy and pious behavior, you who await and hasten towards the coming of the day of God, by which the heavens, being on fire, will be dissolved and the elements will melt away by reason of the heat of the fire. But we look for new heavens and a new earth, according to his promises, wherein dwells justice. Therefore, beloved, while you look for these things, endeavor to be found by him without spot and blameless, in peace. And regard the long-suffering of our Lord as salvation (2 Pet. 3:3–15).

Our outlook today is quite different from that of the early Christians for whom St. Peter wrote, and there can be no question of our adopting their exaggerated eschatologism. But we cannot ignore the fact that the whole history of the Church lies between the two comings of Christ, and that the entire life of the Church on earth, and hence the life of each Christian, unfolds between these two points in history. If the Christian wants really to belong to the Church, he must go beyond a preoccupation with his own individual destiny, or rather, he must never separate his personal destiny from the great movement which carries the Church down through the centuries. By his baptism, and by the grace which lives in him, which shapes him and which, through him, shapes the world, he is part of the developing kingdom, and he must build up this kingdom by his daily life and thus work toward the final end, the fulfillment of the redemption by the eternal triumph of Christ on the last day. Then, on that day chosen by God, the date of which no one on earth knows, everything will be ready for the final crowning of the blessed. Then he will be able to say that he "hastened" the coming of the Lord.

Thus the three aspects of the Christian Advent are joined into a wonderful unity—the coming of Christ the Messias, who merited salvation for us and who inaugurated the earthly phase of the kingdom; the coming of Christ into our souls by grace; and lastly, our awaiting, with the whole Church, our Lord's return in glory to establish His eternal kingdom.

·∘[8]∘·

Sins against Hope

✠

In medio stat virtus: it is the function of virtue to mark out the proper bounds in everything. Sin always originates in a lack of due measure, for we sin against a virtue whenever we do not observe proper limits either by excess or by defect. But can we say that even the theological virtues must keep within certain limits? Actually, they transcend all human boundaries since they have as object the Infinite God. Therefore, as regards their object, they cannot be excessive, for we can never believe or hope in God as much as we ought, nor can we ever love Him as much as He should be loved. As St. Bernard says, "The measure of the love of God is to love Him without measure."

Nevertheless, it is we who practice these virtues, we who are in well-defined circumstances, bound by our limitations and the laws of our nature. In this respect we can speak of due measure in the practice of the theological virtues. Our hope, then, must respect the limitations of our condition as men. It must follow the golden mean between defect and excess—defect, if we do not attain the hope to which we are called; excess, if we presume to go beyond the permitted bounds of hope. The former is the sin of despair; the latter, the sin of presumption.

1. Despair

This is not the place to make a phenomenological study of despair, although such a study would be extremely interesting. Instead, we shall confine ourselves to a short description of the sin of despair.

We must be on our guard against confusing despair with certain attitudes or feelings which are often wrongly identified with it. Despair is not that pessimism which some people affect or really experience when they reflect on world events or their own lives. Nor is it the simple discouragement which sometimes descends upon the best of us in times of trial. It does not consist in lack of drive or the simple waning of confident fervor, or in the anguish which even the saints felt when they compared their imperfection with the infinite greatness of God.

In addition, there is a type of despair that is not a real contradiction of theological hope. For example, we may have wanted something with our whole heart—success, the cure of an illness, the victory of a good cause, the requital of love, etc. We have hoped for it with all our strength, and circumstances, indifference, or injustice have dashed our hopes so that we are left in "despair." With "death in our soul," we are compelled to forego the happiness we desired so much. Life contains many occasions of such despair as this. However, there is no question here of losing essential hope because we do not despair of God, which is the sin against hope. Theological hope primarily throws us into God's arms as into the arms of one who can do everything and who loves us. It makes us throw ourselves on Him even, so to say, before we expect from Him anything at all, for we must first hope *in* God before hoping *for* Him. Therefore, the sin against hope consists in despairing *of* God.

Despair, like every grave sin, must be a conscious and fully deliberate act. It is the deliberate refusal of eternal happiness, a clean break with beatitude. Yet the despairing man does not necessarily stop desiring happiness. On the contrary, he continues to aspire to it with all his strength, and his whole being cries out for it. However—and this is what causes his heartbreak—he is convinced that he can never attain the happiness he desires. Despair therefore has all the marks of a definitive renouncement and abandonment. To despair is to reject God and refuse His goodness, omnipotence, and love; it means to reject the supernatural destiny which He proposes to men. Holy Scripture offers us many examples of despair; from Cain, who cried: "My punishment is too great to bear" (Gen. 4:13), and went out into the wilderness, to Judas, who despaired of being pardoned and hanged himself.

Correctly, then, despair does not consist in the mere temptation to imagine that God has abandoned us forever but rather in the accepted conviction that He has done so because our sins are too grave and the divine mercy is exhausted (as if Christ had not already paid the full ransom for our sins!), because our weakness and the response that evil finds in us have closed the door to a true Christian life (as if grace were not efficacious!), or because we see in the trials of life a sign that we are accursed (as if we held the false views of Job's "comforters" or believed that God desires death for the sinner and not life!).

We can sin also in despairing of the fate of mankind. Certainly, the shocking assertion of evil and injustice in the world, the appalling future that lies in store for us if the prodigious advances in science are misused, as is always possible—humanly speaking, all this can make us despair. However, true despair is a loss of hope *in God* when we are confronted with difficulties; it is a condemnation and malediction of the world as a whole, as if the forces of evil could finally prevail over God's love!

Some may object that despair is not possible without a previous lessening of the faith whereby we believe in God's love, infinite goodness, and help. If we believe in God, then how can we despair? In reality, faith can exist in a soul given over to despair. Of course, despair involves a false idea of God's mercy, yet this wrong idea can leave faith intact. The despairing man can really believe that God is infinitely good, that He wills the salvation of all men, and that He forgives sins (a conviction that springs from faith). But when he comes to make a practical judgment in his own case, his logic fails and he regards himself as not sharing in the common destiny of believers. He refuses to apply to himself the infinite goodness of God; he turns away from it and withdraws into his powerless misery. This is the tragedy of a faith that remains unfruitful; it is the cruel illogicality of a faith that is not living.

Who can doubt, then, that despair is a sin and one of the gravest sins, at that? For isn't it a spurning of the most precious gifts that God has placed at the service of men—His power, His goodness and the merits of Christ, which can compensate for any sin? In themselves, refusal of faith or hatred of God are graver sins than despair, the former because it is in direct opposition to divine truth, and the latter because it repays God's love with hate. Yet despair is, from a psychological point of view, perhaps the most dangerous and terrible of sins. The man given over to despair has nothing left to cling to. Everything that could give any value or fervor to his life has vanished, and he is left with only a feeling of complete frustration, of having lost irretrievably the most powerful incentive to action, a sense of happiness. That is why, as experience shows, despair logically leads to suicide, in which the despairing man becomes a victim of the ultimate and most monstrous of aberrations by seeking an annihilation which he shall never find.

2. Rebellion

In our opinion, rebellion against God should be bracketed with dsepair. By rebellion we mean here conscious, stubborn rebellion and not those instinctive, almost uncontrollable reactions of a soul that remains fundamentally submissive to God as described, for example, in the Book of Job. Real rebellion against God is rather that downright obstinacy in revolt, that attitude of systematic refusal of

complete confidence in Him and of recourse to His omnipotence which goes with despair and which is, as it were,
its inseparable companion in some sections of contemporary
literature.

Pride is always at the back of rebellion. The proud man,
thinking he is a level-headed conservative, declares: "Perhaps I shall not amount to very much, but whatever I'm
going to achieve, I'll achieve by myself." The rebellious
man says: "I don't want anything from God, either pity or
grace. I want to solve my own problems and those of the
world all by myself even if I must end up in complete despair." Undoubtedly such a man is presumptuous, but, even
worse, he is setting out on a hopeless mission and he knows
it's hopeless.

3. Discouragement

Discouragement is less serious than despair or rebellion because it is not a rejection of God; yet it is in the same
general category. While it is not the death of hope, it is a
sickness, an anemia of hope. It can, and often does, come
from physical or moral lassitude. But this lassitude, which
is caused by the experience of failure and of the necessity
to keep on making new beginnings, can cause a lessening
of hope to such a point that we no longer want to wait for
God's saving and strengthening grace, that we no longer
have any confidence in ourselves. This lack of self-confi-
dence is good but only up to a certain point, for it can be
and often is simply the obverse of our lack of confidence
in God. We feel keenly that we are the poorest of the poor
but we forget the dimension that gives poverty the spiritual and religious character which marked "Yahweh's poor

ones" and which our Lord emphasized in the Beatitudes, namely, total, confident abandonment to God's goodness and grace. We repeat: the Christian's bitter knowledge of his misery, while it removes any illusory confidence in his own strength, should serve only to plunge him the more deeply into abandonment to the all-powerful tenderness of his God.

The same must be said of that systematic pessimism which disparages everything, which sees only evil in all things and which—due regard being had for different temperaments—rests on a purely human point of view.

PRESUMPTION

1. Presumption

The opposite of despair is presumption. The malice of presumption, however, is less apparent than that of despair. Nevertheless, presumption is a direct contradiction of hope because it renders inordinate the soul's movement toward beatitude. It is a disorderly act of the will which tries to attain an end beyond the limits assigned by God. Like despair, it is often born of pride, which is the source of every inordinate sentiment.

The excess called presumption can take either of two forms. In the first, presumption urges us to wish to attain eternal happiness without God, and relying solely on our own strength. It makes us so foolishly confident in our strength, worth, and excellence that we try to gain, by will power alone, the happiness for which we are destined, and thereby it closes to us every road to the end we are pursuing.

The other form of presumption is still worse, for it is an evil deformation of confidence in God. In this type of presumption we do not refuse God's help but, on the contrary, expect unreasonable and impossible things from Him. The presumptuous man expects everything from God and does nothing himself; he wants to obtain from God the fruit of His promises without fulfilling the conditions they demand. This is the capital error in Luther's doctrine which deforms confidence in God to the extent that it expects the predestined to be rewarded with heaven no matter how great their vices or profligacy. "Sin strongly but believe more strongly," as Luther himself put it. This is the presumption of those who believe that God is too "good" to punish sin, while they forget that, of itself, God's goodness is a condemnation of evil. They try to obtain forgiveness without being sorry for their sins. St. Thomas regards this presumption as a sin against the Holy Ghost.

2. Passive Optimism

Just as pessimism is connected with despair, so also is passive or ineffectual optimism linked with presumption. There are some Christians who are almost incurably pessimistic and who are always torturing themselves with gloomy forebodings. If they were presented with happiness on a silver platter, they would push it aside so that they might go on being miserable. And there are others who are incurable optimists: their motto is, "Everything will turn out all right by itself." Experience only serves to strengthen their optimism since not all the events of life are tragic. When an enterprise which he has undertaken only halfheartedly fails, the pessimist exclaims: "I told you so!" In like manner, when certain problems are solved or disappear because of circumstances or the mere passage of time, the optimist also cries: "I told you so!" And we're lucky if he doesn't claim all the credit!

There is a kind of confidence in life that can sin by excess, but true hope has no element of smug, lazy optimism. Rather it is dynamic, an inspiration to act, like the very power of God that flows through us, the power of God who acts in us, through and with us. In the progressive realization of hope, we are not just spectators, but are, by the grace of God, active participants.

··❧[9]❧··

Hope and Our World

✠

CONTINUITY OR BREAK?

We should like to devote this last chapter to a considera-
tion of the most pressing and most discussed problem in the
theology of hope, namely, what bearing has our hope on
the present world? We shall not try to seek a solution but
shall merely make a modest attempt to see where we stand.

The problem has been stated in concrete terms and in
very different yet converging ways. The Christian engaged
in everyday activities asks himself rather anxiously: "Isn't
everything we do in this world, especially in the area of
temporal values such as in the technological, cultural, political, economic and social spheres—isn't everything of
temporary value only?" Of course, he knows that, as a

child of God in the state of grace, he stores up merit for eternal life in everything he does. But isn't the very substance, the raw material, as it were, upon which man exerts so much effort, doomed to ultimate annihilation? The Christian doctor or scholar can legitimately ask if he would not be better off if he consecrated a large part of his life to prayer rather than to relieving pain or searching out the secrets of the universe. We may object and say that the performance of the duties of our state in life is an essential element of our Christian vocation. But that does not solve our problem: it merely shifts it.

Has this temporal work any value for eternity? Is there a continuity between our present efforts and the future, eschatological world, which is the essential object of hope? And pushing the question to its limits, do men lose for eternity their efforts to improve world conditions when they exert those efforts while they are not in the state of grace? Here we are faced with some important aspects of a theology of work, for example, with a Christian concept of humanism and, in a word, with all that concerns the theology of the laity. We come up against one of the most debated problems of our times under its very varied titles— a theology of history, of sacred and secular history, a theology of temporal values, of optimism or pessimism. All these questions can be reduced to one: is there a break or a continuity between our world and the world to come? In other words, is the relationship between this life and the next "a mere relationship of exterior conditioning, or is it a relationship of intrinsic and organic continuity?"[1]

[1] L. Malevez, *La vision chrétienne de l'histoire*, II; *Dans la théologie catholique*, in *Nouvelle Revue Théologique*, 1949, No. 3, p. 244. The

Expressing the problem in terms of a theology of hope, we may ask: "Can we hope for at least the embryonic but still substantial establishment of the kingdom of God in our world?"

OPPOSITE TRENDS

In Catholic theology on this subject there are two sometimes violently conflicting trends, while in Protestant theology there are three such trends. We shall examine the Protestant positions first.

1. In Protestant Theology

The second general assembly of the World Council of Churches held at Evanston, Illinois, in 1954 took as its theme, "Christ, the hope of the world." At this assembly many differences of opinion were brought to light, differ-

---

bibliography on these problems is abundant. For the Catholic viewpoint, see also L. Malevez's other articles in *Nouvelle Revue Théologique*, especially his *Philosophie chrétienne du progrès, ibid.*, 1937, p. 381, and his book, *The Christian Message and Myth*, translated by O. Wyon (Westminster, Md.: Newman, 1958); Y. Congar, *Lay People in the Church* (Westminster, Md.: Newman, 1959); G. Thils, *Théologie des réalités terrestres*, 1949; D. Dubarle, *Optimisme devant ce monde*, 1949; J. Daniélou, *Christianisme et histoire*, in *Études*, Sept., 1947; R. Aubert, *Discussions récentes, autour de la théologie de l'histoire*, in *Collectanea Mechliniensia*, 1948, pp. 129-149; P. Teilhard de Chardin, *The Phenomenon of Man*, trans. by B. Wall (New York: Harper and Brothers, 1959). Among the numerous studies of Fr. Teilhard de Chardin's thought, C. Tresmontant's *Pierre Teilhard de Chardin, His Thought* (Baltimore: Helicon Press, 1959); D. Dubarle's article, *A propos du phénomène humain du P. Teilhard de Chardin*, in *La Vie Intellectuelle*, March, 1936, and A. Delcourt's *La vision scientifique du monde*, in *La Revue Nouvelle*, 1958, No. 6, are especially noteworthy.

ences which, in general, can be traced to three trends. The first concentrates hope exclusively on the end of the world and holds that hope should be defined in its relationship with the *parousia* or glorious return of the Son of Man. The second view, while not denying Christ's return, teaches that eschatology does not hold an essential place in Christian hope, and that hope looks to the present time and the establishment of the kingdom now. We should recall here how the first Christians' expectation of Christ's immediate return was not fulfilled, and how dangerous it is to take the eschatological terms in the Bible too literally.[2] Finally there is the middle position according to which hope cannot be defined solely in terms of the expectation of Christ's return since the actual presence of Christ and the gift of the Holy Spirit are elements of hope.[3]

The principal aim of the report upon which these discussions were based was to show the relevance of hope for the present day. After a quick comparison of Christian

[2] A. Schweitzer, for example, holds that Christ was "deluded," that He was mistaken about the imminence of the world's end; therefore, he says, the eschatology of the New Testament is obviously wrong and must be completely abandoned by modern Christians. Faithful to his principles and with admirable generosity, Schweitzer has devoted his whole life to an attempt at putting into effect a kind of philanthropic humanism in the present world.

[3] These three tendencies embrace very divergent concepts. The first is primarily that of the Adventist sects. Under the second we can class theologians or philosophers as different as C. H. Dodd ("realized eschatology") and R. Bultmann, who advocates a "demythologization" of the New Testament in favor of an existentialist interpretation of the Gospel message. The middle position is taken especially by R. Otto, W. G. Kümmel, O. Cullmann. A survey of the varying positions appears in W. Schweitzer, *Eschatology and Ethics* (Ecumenical Studies, Geneva, 1951), and in G. J. Heering, *De verwachtung van het Koninkrijk Gods* (Arnhem, 1952).

hope with the contemporary Utopias, which were reduced to three principal forms, Stalinism, scientific humanism and the democratic Utopia, the report analyzed the relationship of hope to the Christian vocation in the world. Christ has brought us peace, justice, freedom, life, and truth, whence come our moral obligations to act in the world. Because we possess peace now and at the same time hope for eternal peace, we must work to restore temporal peace in a threatened and divided world. Because we have justice, we must fight for justice among men and must oppose every form of injustice. Because we enjoy liberty in Christ, we must struggle for freedom on earth and intervene wherever the liberty of man is threatened. Because we have life in Christ, we cannot allow millions of people to be consigned to death while we eat our fill. Because Christ is the truth, we must encourage every search for truth. This is certainly a stirring, but also a rather oversimplified, transposition of hope to the temporal plane. No doubt, the tasks mentioned are truly the Christian's duties in this world, but the problem is to know if Christ's promise, upon which Christian hope is based, allows us to expect in the name of revealed hope that such concrete effects will take place here on earth and that they will continue into eternity.

The independent theologian, Karl Barth, resolutely holds that there is a break between this world and the next: [4]

Barth repeats unceasingly that our true being cannot appear here below and that the very faith "which makes us accept

[4] For an excellent study of Barth's thought on this point see L. Malevez, *La vision chrétienne de l'histoire*, I: *Dans la théologie de Karl Barth* in *Nouvelle Revue Théologique*, 1949, No. 2, pp. 113-134.

life calmly, robs us of that calm." By means of this dialectical language Barth wishes to show us the necessary preponderance of our desire for eternity over our participation in time. The Christian should gather up into a great love all the tasks of life because these tasks enable him to glorify God by restoring to the world's ravaged face the image of its Creator. Yet at the very moment of his most intense commitment he must above all be alert to cultivate pure hope within himself. He should keep himself in a state of readiness for a clear-cut miracle, for a "vertical" event [5] (vertical in relation to the horizontal development of history), an event to which his efforts can contribute nothing by themselves and which remains within God's omnipotent power and at the free disposal of His will. However, we are absolutely sure that this event, this miracle, will happen because God, who is faithful to His word, has promised it to us in Christ. . . .[6]

"A special and even essential" feature of Barth's theology of earthly values

is that it rejects the least ontological continuity between the contributions of our present life and the kingdom of God. It denies any proportion between our present existence and eschatological existence, and even any intrinsic predisposition of the former toward the latter. . . .[7]

2. In Catholic Theology

There are two very distinct trends among Catholic theologians: the eschatological trend, an example of which we have seen in Barth,[8] and the evolutionary trend, also called

[5] "Das reine absolute vertikale Wunder," *Der Römerbrief*, p. 35.
[6] L. Malevez, *loc. cit.*, pp. 130–131.
[7] *Ibid.*, p. 134.
[8] This trend is found in the writings of Frs. Bouyer and Daniélou, for example.

the "incarnation" theory, which, on the theological plane, is akin to the theories of Fr. Teilhard de Chardin in the realm of science.[9]

1. The Eschatological Tendency

By stressing the return of Christ on the last day and the break that it will mark, this viewpoint places the accent on the discontinuity of this world with the next.

> Human effort and man's contribution to world progress have a relationship to the final, definitive reality, the kingdom of God . . . but there is no continuity between them. The kingdom of God is not the result of world progress, but, according to the Bible, appears as already given and as residing essentially in Christ's power. Strictly speaking, neither the world nor the Church brings the kingdom to pass. Instead it is given from on high, and only Christ, by *His* power, will establish it.[10]

Even without an appeal to the Apocalypse, this position can be supported by New Testament texts referring to the *parousia*, texts which seem to foretell a complete cosmic upheaval or the dissolution of the present world (Matt. 24, 2 Pet. 3:7, 10–12), which will then be replaced by a new world, a kingdom from on high (Matt. 25:24). Certain mysterious utterances of our Lord also imply that the eschatological kingdom cannot come as the result of the harmonious development of the moral and religious evolution of the world of men, that the kingdom cannot come from the world as the fruit grows from the flower. On the

[9] G. Thils and L. Malevez are notable advocates of this trend.
[10] Y. Congar, *Pour une théologie du laïcat*, in *Études*, 1948, pp. 213f. Fr. Congar has developed his views in greater detail in his book.

contrary, our Lord sometimes seems to stress the opposition that the eschatological kingdom will meet: "Yet when the Son of Man comes, will he find, do you think, faith on earth?" (Luke 18:8); "The charity of the many will grow cold" (Matt. 24:12). Furthermore, there seems to be an irreducible contradiction between the Gospel and "the world," this world which is stained by sin, and has persecuted the disciples of Christ; this world which even in its cosmic dimensions has been subjected to sin by man's will (*cf*. Rom. 8:20). In short, sin must be taken seriously.[11]

All this warrants a reasonable doubt of the possibility that our world will change smoothly into the world to come. On the contrary, the evidence points quite clearly to the idea of a break and an upheaval.

2. The Evolutionary Tendency

At the other extreme, the philosophy of Fr. Teilhard de Chardin, for example, looks toward a harmonious evolution. Fr. Teilhard de Chardin was not a theologian but rather a scientist who believed that, in the constant elements of the evolution of the universe, he had found principles that allow us to foretell the future of humanity. When, as far as is possible, we review with him the evolution of the universe and the appearance of "the phenomenon of man," and when we perceive the law of continuous, unremitting progress, we can scarcely help being enchanted by the gigantic perspective that is opened up before us, and we are moved to ask why must the progress stop short? Energy first evolved into living things which then evolved into

[11] See P. Bouyer's very definite views in his article *Christianisme et eschatologie*, in *La Vie Intellectuelle* (Oct., 1948, pp. 6–38).

man. Why cannot this line of evolution continue so that
mortal man will evolve into eternal man? Is not God, the
Alpha of creation, also its Omega?

> [Fr. Teilhard de Chardin] is trying to find out, first,
> toward which crucial frontier humanity is travelling, and
> then, what will result when that frontier is reached. . . .
> Men talk to each other and understand each other through-
> out the world. All problems are posed on a world scale.
> Humanity tends to become increasingly social-minded, and
> there is a world-wide meeting of minds. A new kind of com-
> plexity has arisen from which a fusion more intimate than
> all the others should develop. Each man will find his place
> there and will contribute his personal part to the building up
> of the new world, the world of love where God will be
> definitively all in all. As in the preceding stages, the new level
> will be attained, not by a simple meeting of individuals, but
> by a fusion of souls through love, a fusion so intimate that
> all will belong vitally to the same Body, of which Christ be-
> came the Head by His Incarnation and in which the world
> finds again its divine origin.[12]

The theologians who follow the evolutionary trend have
certainly been influenced, consciously or unconsciously,
by Fr. Teilhard de Chardin's views, yet they defend their
positions on the authority of theological principles. Need-
less to say, these positions are quite subtle. However, they
are sometimes expressed in very clear terms:

> If these views are correct, it follows that, by themselves,
> contemporary mastery over matter, political organization, art,
> thought and all technologies complete Christ and thereby

[12] A. Delcourt, *loc. cit.,* pp. 609–610.

glorify Him. And they do so independently of the good or evil intentions which inspire them.[13]

This theological position stresses the reality of the Incarnation (the Son of God made flesh and remaining eternally the Man-God), its extension to the whole economy of salvation, and the assurance that we have of possessing even now a pledge of the future kingdom in the unceasing action of the Holy Spirit in our world.

While affirming the continuity between the Church and the kingdom on the plane of *sacred history*, Fr. Malevez sets down the limits of this continuity.[14] First of all, our actions as Christians, by their very nature and insofar as they are merely our actions, lack intrinsic value for heaven.

> If, therefore, God gives Himself to us after this life as a continuation of our works, His gift will not correspond to the merely human substance of those works (*secundum substantiam operis*) but to the supernatural and mystical quality with which God Himself will have endowed them here on earth.

Furthermore the reign of sin has not yet been completely broken. In the Christian there persist "whole regions where self remains stubbornly aloof from, and even in opposition to, the Holy Spirit." Therefore, if we consider man in himself, "there is a complete ontological discontinuity between his contributions and the kingdom; even more, there is a positive incompatibility between the two as regards our condition as sinners."

[13] L. Malevez, *Philosophie chrétienne du progrès*, in *Nouvelle Revue Théologique*, 1937, p. 381.
[14] *La vision chrétienne de l'histoire*, II: *Dans la théologie catholique*, in *Nouvelle Revue Théologique*, March, 1949, pp. 244–264.

Our actions as Christians are limited also in that their effects are not evident. We believe in the transcendent effects of our actions, but we do not see and cannot prove these effects. Yet they are assured to us by faith. That is why, when we consider the Christian as such,

> as one who has become greater than his natural self with God's help, we discern a perfect continuity between his earthly and his heavenly condition. But this continuity is beyond our powers of observation and reasoning, and we apprehend it only through faith.

To what extent can we recognize a continuity on the plane of *secular history*, at the level of material effort? To quote Fr. Malevez again:

> It would be impious to think that our secular culture could ever produce our heavenly condition by its own power or by an efficacy that is in some way distinctive. Furthermore, in contrast to the "achievements" of Christian history, the highest accomplishments of secular history will never give us the least right or the least need in regard to the new man. Finally, all of man's most spectacular contributions will pale and fade away in the dawn of the last day. Materially speaking, none of the fruits of man's genius will remain. Thus the difference and discontinuity between this world and the next which is expressed in the Scriptures, is assured, and support is given to the contemporary Catholic theologians who favor the eschatological viewpoint. But all of this does not prevent us, on the other hand, from paying due attention to the "perfectionist" trend in theology in keeping with the orientation of Christian thought, and from proclaiming that all the victories of thought and art over the inertia and opacity of matter are so many achievements of Christ Himself, of that Christ for whom Scripture tells us everything was made,

whose sovereignty goes beyond the frontiers of the Church, which is His Body in the strict sense, in order to exert its influence on all the "powers" and upon the whole universe. Thus our purely human actions, insofar as they are not sinful, express Christ, tell of Him and, above all, prepare interiorly for the building up of His Body.[15]

Fr. Malevez is appealing here to the scholastic theory of "disposing forms" which prepare for, but do not demand, substantial forms. These "disposing forms" are, however, necessary for the coming of the substantial forms and are already under their power. He concludes: "We can believe that the City of God will undoubtedly owe some of the features of its final form to the traits and characteristics which the civilizations of history shall have imprinted on our earthly cities."

For his part, G. Thils stresses the action of the Holy Spirit who, combating the influence of the flesh (in the Pauline sense of the word), tends to "spiritualize" everything and, in particular, to lead mankind along difficult and often obstructed paths toward greater organic unity, more universality, peace, freedom, and sanctity. Thils also sees in Christian action as it takes place in history both certain *prefigurings* (images of the final reality which will be actualized only in heaven by God's intervention) such as certain techniques, arts, etc., as well as certain *preludes* or definite works which are even now substantially those which will be achieved later, such as the fruits of charity in particular.

From these principles, Thils draws some practical rules:

[15] *Loc. cit.*, pp. 260–261.

Working in the world and promoting its temporal evolution seems, therefore, to have a meaning. May God grant that this meaning be a Christian one! It can be said that every act which is a "spiritual" contribution to the world truly advances it in the sense willed by Christ and the Holy Spirit. (The word "spiritual" is to be understood in the sense of organic unity, universality, sanctity, peace, etc.) Consequently, Christians engaged in temporal activities can be taught that:

(a) To give more "spirituality" to the evolving world is to cooperate with Christ and the Holy Spirit in the activity they exercise in the secular world as such. This act is therefore "Christian" in a particular sense without necessarily being "meritorious."

(b) When similar activity is performed by one of the faithful in the state of grace, it is, by that very fact, directed toward man's final end and is therefore meritorious. In this case, activity is "Christian" in the full sense of the term.

(c) The "spiritual" values that are contributed to the evolving world, even by a nonmeritorious act, constitute real and genuine progress. A peaceful political regime organized by a person who is not in the state of grace is a real contribution to progress for it is the "worldly" implementation of the gifts of the Holy Spirit by one who, unhappily, is deprived of these gifts.

(d) Real progress can be used for evil ends as well as for good ones. Must progress therefore be avoided? Obviously not. God created man and gave him free will, the ability to choose good or evil, whereas He could have created nothing but stones! Christianity's innate optimism can supply the answer to any doubts in this regard.

(e) On the other hand, to refuse to give the evolving world the leaven of "spirituality" is equivalent to refusing to collaborate with Christ and the Holy Spirit in the secular domain as such. Of course, this collaboration can be done in different ways, directly by those who work "in the world," and indirectly by those who pray for the salvation of the world. But since world evolution is irreversible, to keep aloof from it or to refuse to contribute to it means to oppose it.

Thus the scope of human endeavor, sustained by true, undying hope, is as wide as all creation. The Christian knows that if his visible, earthly action is "spiritual," it is a real contribution to a work which, according to the will of Christ the King and the Holy Spirit, tends to increase and grow unceasingly. True, the primary aspect of theological hope is the expectation of God Himself, since basically we hope for God. But there is no opposition between this hope and the expectation of seeing the establishment of God's domain on earth. Since the coming of Christ, the whole City of God has become the object of theological hope. It is impossible to wait for God without also awaiting, with Him, in Him, and as He does, His absolute, universal reign. Waiting for Him means waiting for that in which He will be all in all. Hence the Christian, without fear or misgivings, should hope for the establishment of God's earthly reign either as a magnificent prefiguring or as a definitive prelude.[16]

SOME BRIDGEHEADS

Is it possible to take sides? Can we give a confident answer to the question: will there be a break or continuity between the present world and the world to come? We believe that hope, based on faith, is, like faith, clothed in mystery. Christ warned us: "You know neither the day nor the hour" (Matt. 25:13), and perhaps we should extend His warning to include not only the time but also the manner of

[16] G. Thils, *Espérance et sens chrétien de l'histoire*, in *Lumen Vitae*, 1954, No. 3, pp. 499–500. This long quotation was necessary to explain, without misrepresentation, the positions taken by "evolutionary" theologians.

the establishment of His kingdom. Still, we can recall several principles which must not be overlooked and which can serve as "bridgeheads" to a solution, if we may be permitted this use of the word.

1. Avoid Every Trace of Manichaeism

The two positions outlined above give rise to two different outlooks on the world—pessimism and optimism. (Or perhaps it's the other way around: the two positions may be begotten of pessimism and optimism respectively, since a theologian's temperament may play a part in fashioning his outlook.) Obviously, eschatologism reveals and supports a rather pessimistic view of the value of this world, while evolutionism follows a very optimistic line of thought.

Is the world good or bad? Is it the kingdom of God already begun or is it instead the anti-Gospel? Here, especially, we must avoid every trace of Manichaeism. It is possible that, while firmly condemning in principle the division of the elements of creation into good and bad (spirit and matter), we nevertheless unconsciously subscribe to that division. Such traces of Manichaeism can appear in the conception we form of the value of the world and of the opposition between flesh and spirit.

Our Lord expressed His opposition to the world in categorical terms: "My kingdom is not of this world" (John 18:36); "Woe to the world because of scandals!" (Matt. 18:7); "You are from below, I am from above. You are of this world, I am not of this world" (John 8:23); "If the world hates you, know that it has hated me before you. If you were of the world, the world would love what is its own. But because you are not of this world, but I have chosen you out of the world, therefore the world hates you" (John 15:18-19); "I pray for them; not for this world do I pray . . . The world has hated them, because they are not of the world, even as I am not of the world. I do not pray that you take them out of the world but that thou keep them from evil" (John 17:9, 14-15). Satan is the prince of the world (cf. John 12:31), and Christ's victory is a victory over the world: "Take courage, I have overcome the world" (John 16:33). So also the Christian who has faith in Christ has conquered the world. "Because all that is born of God overcomes the world; and this is the victory that overcomes the world, our faith. Who is there that overcomes the world if not he who believes that Jesus is the Son of God?" (1 John 5:4-5).

Nevertheless, when God created the world, He reviewed the stages of His work and "saw that it was good." Again, we are told that: "God so loved the world that he gave his only-begotten Son . . . God did not send his Son into the world in order to judge, but that the world might be saved through him" (John 3:16-17). Therefore, the world has two aspects, as coming fresh from God's hands and as vitiated by sin, for it is a world in which God's creation and the malice of men are in some way blended, a world which God loves and wishes to save despite everything.

It is true that the world of sin as such is opposed to God and in contradiction to the kingdom, but it is difficult to untangle the ramifications of evil in the world and to gauge the repercussions of sin on creation. This ambiguity, this paradox is inherent in the world as it is, and even the kingdom itself, in its present stage of development, has the same paradoxical mixture of good and evil (see the parables of the weeds among the wheat, and the net filled with good and bad fish in Matt. 13). Good and evil exist there side by side and mingle with each other. How far, then, can our condemnation of the world go? We must take sin seriously, but how far does sin extend? Is not sin simply man's perverse intention, which he projects into things, into matter, into the energies of the world? What right, then, have we to be suspicious of these things?

The world certainly cannot work out its own salvation or even prepare itself therefore by its own powers. It will owe its salvation only to a free gift of God. But can't it be saved by being purged of sin, in which man involved it, without having to pass through annihilation? If God's creation is good, why should He annihilate it? Purification and redemption are necessary but surely the world can be redeemed and purified without being destroyed?

The opposition between spirit and flesh also seems to be a lingering relic of Manichaeism. We know that in St. Paul the strong opposition between the "carnal" and the "spiritual" is not to be identified with the distinction between the body and the soul, but apparently we have lost too much of the idea of the unity of man and are dreaming of an ideal, eternal man who is completely spiritual, as it were. (We have seen how traditional theology considers the resurrection as a mere "complement" of eternal beatitude.) There again, "the body of sin" or "the body of death" is not the whole of the body. Eternal man, beatified man must remain a man. Hence the importance of the dogma of the resurrection of the body, a dogma which, in practice, is not appreciated enough.[17] Our imaginative representation of a new, completely spiritual world sins perhaps by being too "angelic."

Furthermore, we must distrust the tricks which our imagination plays on us. For a long time it has been customary to represent the origin of the world in a way which, while it does not change the basic idea of creation, does distort and harden it into a certain pattern. In the same way, we form a picture of the world's future and destiny, a picture which is a very poor representation of the reality. It is true that, in order to think, we need the help of mental images, but we must have the intellectual courage to confine these images to their proper role as mere approximations of reality; we must keep them on the periphery of the central idea.

2. Immanence and Transcendence

There is another law of ambiguity which underlies the whole Christian reality. It is found in all God's designs for humanity and it is particularly evident in the mystery of the Incarnation. God, who is completely transcendent, deigned to become "embroiled" with the world even to the extent of having His Son become man. Now, the Incarnation was not a transitory state, for the Son of God will remain man for eternity. And all the extensions of the Incarnation have this double character—grace, which penetrates nature without destroying it; the life of God, which becomes our life; the sacraments, which are tangible signs

[17] After His Resurrection, Christ showed His apostles that He was not a "spirit": "See my hands and feet, that it is I myself. Feel me and see; for a spirit does not have *flesh* and *bones*, as you see I have" (Luke 24:38).

and fleshly carriers of this divine life and which culminate in the Eucharist, the Body of Christ.

This law rules the organic composition of the kingdom, which is both transcendent and immanent, which comes from heaven only because of God's intervention; and which exists already on earth as a gift of God. If we follow this law we must say that the eternal kingdom will not be absolutely different from the kingdom which has already been established among us.

The eschatological events will not bring about a "substantial" change but will manifest with all the vividness of a divine revelation the true visage of redeemed humanity freed at last from everything that had hitherto held it captive. No doubt this change cannot take place without a wrench, a transformation, but it will be like the change of a chrysalis into a butterfly. The divine transcendence will become, as it were, totally immanent at the mysterious culmination of the fulfillment of God's plan, at the occurrence of the great "event."

It is difficult for us now to recognize this eternal visage through the temporal veils that cover it. It is also difficult to know exactly in what respects transcendent eternity is already combined with the "phenomenon" that is our world. But we do know that it is so combined, not because our world can produce the eternal, but because God has placed eternity in our world and will one day reveal it.

How much of the divine transcendence is conveyed by secular history, technology, culture and the sciences? It would be presumptuous to guess: "You will be like God, knowing good and evil!" (Gen. 3:5).

Is not that precisely the lot of our faith, and of our

hope? "Hope that is seen is not hope. For how can a man hope for what he sees?" (Rom. 8:24). This turning to God, who knows what He is doing, how He is leading us, and how He will accomplish His creative work, is also a part of hope.

3. The Criterion of Charity

Everything will pass away, says St. Paul, except charity. Perhaps, then, we shall find the solution to our problem in charity, in the degree of real charity in every human enterprise.

If God is love, then every instance of the immanence of the divine life must also be love or charity. Hence in trying to designate the relationship of our world with the world to come, we shall not choose between external conditioning and perfect continuity, nor shall we even draw a distinction between "prefigurings" and "preludes." Love is the life of God and it is in love, or charity, that this life of God is lived by man on earth as it is in heaven. Hence all that man does is valuable according as it meets the criterion of charity, and no human achievement can escape the rule of charity. Everything man does is for or against charity and hence for or against the eternal kingdom, just as our Lord has warned us that we must either be for Him or against Him.

Earthly values are not free of this law, for to the exact extent that they are in the line of charity and serve the reign of divine love, they contain something of the divine and the eternal. There is therefore no room for using extrinsic classifications and distinguishing between that which is a mere prefiguring or rough sketch which God will tear up before He makes a fair copy and that which is already a substantial beginning. Everything that is not charity directly or by mediation will disappear, and everything that is charity is eternity already begun.

As regards determining now the degree of charity in every human enterprise, that is God's business; that is the Father's secret. We never have evidence as to whether we are worthy of love or of hate, a state of affairs which is characteristic of our earthly condition. Therefore, as long as our pilgrimage lasts, we need hope, which does not deceive.